"Wilkins and Thoennes have p
who want to become acquain
The book is concise and brie̴ ̴ ̴ ̴ ̴ ̴ ̴ ̴ ̴ an astonishing number
of topics. Most importantly, the authors are sure-footed and faithful
guides in both biblical studies and theology."

Thomas R. Schreiner, James Buchanan Harrison Professor of New
Testament, The Southern Baptist Theological Seminary

"A helpful introduction to the world of biblical and theological studies.
Beginning students will find that this little book provides big dividends."

Daniel L. Akin, President, Southeastern Baptist Theological Seminary

"Students seeking the best in evangelical scholarship will find it here.
Profoundly simple and masterfully written, this book will help anyone
wanting to get up to date in theology. Read it with a bowed head and
grateful heart."

Robert E. Coleman, Distinguished Senior Professor of Evangelism and
Discipleship, Gordon-Conwell Theological Seminary

"Wilkins and Thoennes, impressive models of scholarship and teaching
in their own right, have crafted this readable 'preface' as an aid for our
students who are perplexed about the nature and relationship of biblical
studies and theology. The mind fog that can surround these two fields
makes it hard for us to connect the dots for our learners. Thus it can be
difficult to move forward toward a shared passion of what we should do
with the Bible and theology. Wilkins and Thoennes bring texture and
unity to what are often perceived as merely isolated and abstract terms to
be memorized. This book will help enliven the minds and souls of evangelical biblical and theological students and scholars in this generation."

Tim L. Anderson, Professor of Theology, Corban University; author,
What the Bible Says about Intimacy with God

"They say that 'well begun is half done,' and this introduction to biblical
and theological studies will set students up for success from the start.
Wilkins and Thoennes seem to be mind readers as they skillfully antici-
pate and answer so many of the topics, terms, and names that students
will wonder about. A great introduction to a vast field of learning."

Fred Sanders, Professor of Theology, Torrey Honors Institute, Biola
University; author, *The Deep Things of God*

~SERIES ENDORSEMENTS~

BIBLICAL AND
THEOLOGICAL
STUDIES

✚ RECLAIMING THE CHRISTIAN INTELLECTUAL TRADITION

David S. Dockery, series editor

CONSULTING EDITORS

Hunter Baker
Timothy George
Neil Nielson
Philip G. Ryken
Michael J. Wilkins
John D. Woodbridge

OTHER RCIT VOLUMES:

Art and Music, Paul Munson and Joshua Farris Drake
Christian Worldview, Philip G. Ryken
Ethics and Moral Reasoning, C. Ben Mitchell
The Great Tradition of Christian Thinking, David S. Dockery and
    Timothy George
History, Nathan A. Finn
The Liberal Arts, Gene C. Fant Jr.
Literature, Louis Markos
Media, Journalism, and Communication, Read Mercer Schuchardt
The Natural Sciences, John A. Bloom
Philosophy, David K. Naugle
Political Thought, Hunter Baker
Psychology, Stanton L. Jones

BIBLICAL AND THEOLOGICAL STUDIES

A STUDENT'S GUIDE

Michael J. Wilkins and Erik Thoennes

CROSSWAY®

WHEATON, ILLINOIS

Library of Congress Cataloging-in-Publication Data

Names: Wilkins, Michael J., author.
Title: Biblical and theological studies : a studen's guide / Michael J. Wilkins and Erik Thoennes.
Description: Wheaton : Crossway, 2018. | Series: Reclaiming the Christian intellectual tradition | Includes bibliographical references and index.
Identifiers: LCCN 2017040058 (print) | LCCN 2018014533 (ebook) | ISBN 9781433534904 (pdf) | ISBN 9781433534911 (mobi) | ISBN 9781433534928 (epub) | ISBN 9781433534898 (tp)
Subjects: LCSH: Bible—Study and teaching. | Theology—Study and teaching.
Classification: LCC BS600.3 (ebook) | LCC BS600.3 .W5555 2018 (print) | DDC 230.071—dc23

VP			27	26	25	24	23	22	21	20	19	18
15	14	13	12	11	10	9	8	7	6	5	4	3	2	1

To Robert L. Saucy (1930–2015),
a true man of God, faithful friend
and colleague, and exemplary Christian
theologian and gentleman.

CONTENTS

Series Preface   11

Acknowledgments   15

1 Introduction to Biblical and Theological Studies   17

2 Biblical Studies   41

3 Theological Studies   85

Questions for Reflection   111

Glossary   113

Resources for Further Study   117

General Index   122

Scripture Index   125

SERIES PREFACE

The Reclaiming the Christian Intellectual Tradition series is designed to provide an overview of the distinctive way the church has read the Bible, formulated doctrine, provided education, and engaged the culture. The contributors to this series all agree that personal faith and genuine Christian piety are essential for the life of Christ followers and for the church. These contributors also believe that helping others recognize the importance of serious thinking about God, Scripture, and the world needs a renewed emphasis at this time in order that the truth claims of the Christian faith can be passed along from one generation to the next. The study guides in this series will enable believers to see afresh how the Christian faith shapes how we live, how we think, how we write books, how we govern society, and how we relate to one another in our churches and social structures. The richness of the Christian intellectual tradition provides guidance for the complex challenges that believers face in this world.

This series is particularly designed for Christian students and others associated with college and university campuses, including faculty, staff, trustees, and other various constituents. The contributors to the series will explore how the Bible has been interpreted in the history of the church, as well as how theology has been formulated. They will ask: How does the Christian faith influence our understanding of culture, literature, philosophy, government, beauty, art, or work? How does the Christian intellectual tradition help us understand truth? How does the Christian intellectual tradition shape our approach to education? We believe that this series is not only timely but that it meets an important need, because the secular culture in which we now find ourselves is, at best, indifferent to the Christian faith, and the Christian world—at least in its more popular forms—tends to be confused about the beliefs, heritage, and tradition associated with the Christian faith.

At the heart of this work is the challenge to prepare a generation of Christians to think Christianly, to engage the academy and the culture, and to serve church and society. We believe that both the breadth and the depth of the Christian intellectual tradition need to be reclaimed, revitalized, renewed, and revived for us to carry this work forward. These study guides will seek to provide a framework to help introduce students to the great tradition of Christian thinking, seeking to highlight its importance for understanding the world, its significance for serving both church and society, and its application for Christian thinking and learning. The series is a starting point for exploring important ideas and issues such as truth, meaning, beauty, and justice.

We trust that the series will help introduce readers to the apostles, church fathers, Reformers, philosophers, theologians, historians, and a wide variety of other significant thinkers. In addition to well-known leaders such as Clement, Origen, Augustine, Thomas Aquinas, Martin Luther, and Jonathan Edwards, readers will be pointed to William Wilberforce, G. K. Chesterton, T. S. Eliot, Dorothy Sayers, C. S. Lewis, Johann Sebastian Bach, Isaac Newton, Johannes Kepler, George Washington Carver, Elizabeth Fox-Genovese, Michael Polanyi, Henry Luke Orombi, and many others. In doing so, we hope to introduce those who throughout history have demonstrated that it is indeed possible to be serious about the life of the mind while simultaneously being deeply committed Christians.

These efforts to strengthen serious Christian thinking and scholarship will not be limited to the study of theology, scriptural interpretation, or philosophy, even though these areas provide the framework for understanding the Christian faith for all other areas of exploration. In order for us to reclaim and advance the Christian intellectual tradition, we must have some understanding of the tradition itself. The volumes in this series seek to explore this tradition and its application for our twenty-first-century world. Each volume contains a glossary, study questions, and a list of resources for further study, which we trust will provide helpful guidance for our readers.

I am deeply grateful to the series editorial committee: Timothy George, John Woodbridge, Michael Wilkins, Niel Nielson, Philip Ryken, and Hunter Baker. Each of these colleagues joins me in thanking our various contributors for their fine work. We all express our appreciation to Justin Taylor, Jill Carter, Allan Fisher, Lane Dennis, and the Crossway team for their enthusiastic support for the project. We offer the project with the hope that students will be helped, faculty and Christian leaders will be encouraged, institutions will be strengthened, churches will be built up, and, ultimately, that God will be glorified.

Soli Deo Gloria
David S. Dockery
Series Editor

ACKNOWLEDGMENTS

I (Erik) would like to thank my gracious, brilliant wife, Donna, for her steadfast love and support; my precious children, Caroline, Paige, Sam, and Isaac—you make me laugh and bring me great joy; my parents for praying for me; the saints at Grace Evangelical Free Church of La Mirada, California—it is an honor to seek Christ together with you; the deans and faculty of Talbot School of Theology for your collegial humility, integrity, and commitment to the authority of Scripture; my students at Wheaton College and Biola University with whom I have been edified and blessed as we have sought to know Christ together over the past twenty-two years; and David Dockery and Justin Taylor, who were wonderfully kind and helpful in the process of completing this book. I'm honored to write this book with Michael Wilkins, who is an outstanding example to me of a man who knows and walks with Jesus. And it is, of course, Jesus who deserves all the ultimate honor and praise.

———

I (Michael) am grateful to God for my students over the past forty years at Talbot School of Theology, Biola University, who have been central in the writing of this book, because they have been the drawing board on which we have learned to sketch the themes of biblical studies and theology. The opportunity to teach these topics is an incomparable privilege and gift from God.

Likewise the past forty-five years of marriage to my dear wife, Lynne, who has been my best friend and companion in the journey, have been an incomparable blessing and gift from God, as have been our daughters—Wendy, and her husband Jason, and Michelle, and her husband Dan—and our granddaughters, Melia and Ava. Our lives would be much hollower without their joy.

I extend deep thankfulness for the kindness and diligence of David Dockery and Justin Taylor at Crossway for their leadership in guiding this book to see life. And special thanks goes to my research assistant Tina Hsu, now a missionary in Asia, who has a wonderful heart and exegetical acumen. She gave special attention to reading the manuscript and offering excellent insights all along the way and did primary research with reference to recent phenomena in biblical studies.

My fellow faculty and deans and staff have joined together in the quest to make Talbot School of Theology a true community that loves, supports, and spurs each other on to godliness and rigorous scholarship. You likewise are a gift from God. Within this community is the archetypal Erik Thoennes, with whom I have been privileged to join in writing this book. He has a rare and carefully developed balance of mind and heart, which I trust will bless and stimulate all who read these words.

1

INTRODUCTION TO BIBLICAL AND THEOLOGICAL STUDIES

God has spoken. This whole book is about those three simple words. That God has personally, truthfully, and sufficiently revealed himself in the Bible is *the* assumption of our understanding of the study of the Bible. That God is and that he has revealed himself are the most foundational beliefs of a Christian. If there is no God (atheism), or if there is a God but he does not personally reveal himself or get involved with creation (deism), then true knowledge of God is not possible. Our efforts to find answers to life's big questions would then be limited to human experience and speculation. We would be limited to doing "theology from below." But in the very first verse of the Bible, we are taught that God is and that he is the Creator. Then, the phrase "God said" occurs ten times in the first chapter of the Bible (Genesis 1), and when God creates human beings, he blesses and immediately talks to us and invites us to join with him in ruling and creating. Indeed, there is no greater blessing he could give than relating to us—he is our greatest blessing. That is the main reason he made us in the first place—to know and enjoy him. The God of the Bible, then, is not a mere projection of human longings or an absentee landlord, but a God who powerfully creates and meaningfully relates. He is a God who speaks, and his word blesses, provides, and saves us.

These basic assumptions about God undergird the way we

approach biblical studies and theology. The Bible reveals who God is, and that understanding of God then informs how we approach the Bible—as the words of an all-wise, all-powerful, gracious, kind, forgiving, holy, righteous Father and King. We are to fully trust and obey his Word, because of the integrity of its author. The goal is to know the author by listening to his life-giving voice. What we learn, even in an "academic" study of the Bible and theology, should lead to knowledge that unites head, heart, hands, and feet in a holistic, life-changing encounter with our Creator.

Before proceeding any further, it would no doubt be helpful at this point to briefly define what we mean by biblical studies and theology, what the difference is between the two, and why we even make the distinction. *Biblical studies* is an academic discipline that seeks to understand the Bible as God intended when he inspired its human authors. The *study of theology* is the effort to summarize the overall teaching of the Bible so it can be meaningfully applied to our lives. Biblical studies provides the understanding of the biblical text so that we can do the theological task of synthesizing what the Bible teaches so that its teaching can inform and influence every area of life.

As we read the Bible, we find that it has an amazingly unified voice and coherent message, even though forty human authors wrote it over about a two-thousand-year period. These authors were from three different continents and from drastically different walks of life: fisherman, king, shepherd, scholar, and priest are just some of the vocations that writers of the Bible had. They were often addressing very different concerns and very different audiences. With this approach to writing a book, it is hard to imagine that you could ever get an integrated, consistent understanding of things. We not only get that, however; we get an unfolding story that explains all of reality with wonderful truthfulness. This story has all the elements of every great story, and this story has not just explained the world as we know it, it has profoundly shaped the world in which we live.

There is an abundant need today for biblically grounded, clear, concise, practically applied theology. The study of theology must focus on the main issues that God himself emphasizes in the Bible, not on speculative areas we may think important. We must go to God to find not only the right answers, but also the right questions. If we allow our quest for truth to be limited by the latest fads, trends, and pressing issues of the day, we won't get to the most important, God-centered, eternally important questions. Jesus taught us to seek God's kingdom and righteousness and then trust God to supply the lesser things that tend to dominate our thoughts (Matt. 6:33–34).

Most of our students throughout the years grew up in the church. When they dive in to the study of the Bible and learn the foundational truths of their faith, many of them are often astonished that they never *really* learned these things before. Perhaps they were taught the Bible well, but for some reason it never sunk in. Yet, it does seem that over the years there has been less and less of an emphasis on studying the Bible and learning basic doctrine in many churches. It seems that cultural influences have had a detrimental effect on the perceived value of knowing the Bible and its major themes. Pragmatism, consumerism, and an entertainment mentality have shifted the priorities of some churches away from our primary calling to devote ourselves to knowing God deeply through his Word. We need an attitude adjustment and reorientation of our priorities back to our main calling to know God according to the Scriptures.

ATTITUDES FOR DOING BIBLICAL AND THEOLOGICAL STUDIES

Now that we have discussed *why* we study the Bible and theology, we need to consider *how* we study. Much of this book will be about the proper methods of studying the Bible and theology. But *how* we study begins with the state of our hearts. Motives and heart attitudes are of utmost importance. You can be intellectually brilliant and highly knowledgeable, and yet be spiritually dead and unwise. Your basic beliefs, assumptions, and attitudes will determine how you approach your quest for truth. How you define God, humans, and the purpose of life will shape your experience in learning and also determine your methods of learning. So how should the Christian approach the study of the Bible and theology? Here are six helpful attitudes to have when approaching Biblical studies:

(1) We should study the Bible with *fear and worship of God*. God is the greatest thing we could ever try to comprehend. He is perfect in all his ways and staggeringly glorious. When people truly catch but a glimpse of his greatness, they are overwhelmed and forever changed. When Isaiah beheld God's glory in the temple, he said, "Woe is me! For I am lost; for I am a man of unclean lips, and I dwell in the midst of a people of unclean lips; for my eyes have seen the King, the LORD of hosts!" (Isa. 6:5). When Job considered God's majesty in creation, even in the midst of his great trials he said, "I had heard of you by the hearing of the ear, but now my eye sees you; therefore I despise myself, and repent in dust and ashes" (Job 42:5–6). When Peter saw the miraculous power of Christ, he said, "Depart from me, for I am a sinful man, O Lord" (Luke 5:8). True knowledge of God always produces worshipful awe.

After one of the greatest prolonged teachings on theology in the Bible, Paul bursts into praise "Oh, the depth of the riches and wisdom and knowledge of God! How unsearchable are his judgments and how inscrutable his ways! . . . For from him and through him and to him are all things. To him be glory forever. Amen" (Rom. 11:33, 36). Our theology (right thinking) should always lead to doxology (right worship) and orthopraxy (right practice), or else we have a major disconnect in our theology. On the other hand, if our worship and practice are not grounded in deep theology, worship will be shallow, fleeting sentimentality, and its practice will be merely empty moralism. We never need to fear that our awe will deplete because God is infinite and offers an endless supply of data for our worship and fear of him. The adventure of knowing God provides never-ending vistas of glory. Scottish preacher Alexander Whyte beautifully summarized the God-exalting purpose of our study of the Bible:

> First of all, my child, think magnificently of God. Magnify his providence; adore his power, pray to him frequently and incessantly. Bear him always in your mind. Teach your thoughts to reverence him in every place for there is no place where he is not. Therefore, my child, fear and worship and love God; first and last, think magnificently of him![1]

Bursting into praise should be a common occurrence for the student of the Bible. We should follow the example of the inspired authors of Scripture who frequently move from teaching about God's character to unhindered expression of worshipful adoration. One example will have to suffice. After Paul expounds on God's amazing grace to him although he was a former blasphemer, he cannot help but express his gratitude in praise: "To the King of the ages, immortal, invisible, the only God, be honor and glory forever and ever. Amen" (1 Tim. 1:17).

(2) We should study the Bible with *growing humility about ourselves*. As we saw in the previous passages, when we grow in our knowledge of God and we begin to "think magnificently of God," we also grow in humility. A big view of God invariably leads to a small view of ourselves. Studying God's Word shows us a supremely majestic God, and we then learn our place before him. Although we recognize that we are fearfully and wonderfully made in his image, we also know that all we are and have is from his

---

[1] Paternus (a church father from the first century), quoted in Alexander Whyte, *Sermons on Prayer by Alexander Whyte* (London: Hodder and Stoughton, 1922), 6, http://www.ccel.org/ccel/whyte/pray.v.i.html.

hand, and we are but dust before him—glorious dust to be sure, but dust all the same. God is infinite (unlimited) and holy, and we are finite (limited) and fallen. God is the author of life and the source of all that is good. God has no unmet needs and does not need us for anything. "Not is [God] served by human hands, as though he needed anything, since he himself gives to all mankind life and breath and everything" (Acts 17:25).

Everything we have is a gift from his gracious heart. Realizing this stops all human boasting in its tracks. "What do you have that you did not receive? . . . If then you received it, why do you boast as if you did not receive it?" (1 Cor. 4:7).

When we study the Bible, we will at times go beyond others in our knowledge, which could lead to arrogance. This is a heinous but common tendency that God warns about when he tells us that "knowledge puffs up but love builds up" (1 Cor. 8:1). This arrogance can lead to looking down on those who don't know as much as we do, and Helmut Thielicke calls this a spiritual disease that is *the* disease of the theologian.[2] This disease leads to using truth "as a means to personal triumph and at the same time as a means to kill,"[3] which is the opposite of God's intention for learning truth. We are to build others up with our learning, not tear them down. Learning about the greatness of God should lower our own estimation, but sadly this is often not the case. This means we have to go to war with pride every day. *Arrogant* and *Christian* are two words that should never go together. All our boasting should be "in the Lord" (1 Cor. 1:31).

God hates pride. Having too high an estimation of our knowledge is where Adam and Eve got it wrong in the garden, and we have followed their foolishness ever since. The word *sophomore* literally means "wise fool" because, early in our education, we know enough to think we know a lot, but we have not learned enough to

---

[2] Helmut Thielicke, *A Little Exercise for Young Theologians* (Grand Rapids, MI: Eerdmans, 1962), 17.
[3] Thielicke, *A Little Exercise for Young Theologians*, 19.

know how little we really know. Arrogance in our Bible knowledge or theological positions is an abomination to the Lord. We would all be wise, young and old alike, to heed the following admonition from the apostle Peter: "Likewise, you who are younger, be subject to the elders. Clothe yourselves, all of you, with humility toward one another, for 'God opposes the proud but gives grace to the humble'" (1 Pet. 5:5).

(3) We should study with *prayerful dependence on the Holy Spirit*. Atheists can understand the meaning of the Bible. Even demons can have highly accurate theology. James tells us that demons are card-carrying monotheists (James 2:19). So there must be a kind of accurate knowledge that does not necessarily lead to God-honoring adoration, worship, and obedience. The key difference is the work of the Holy Spirit. The truth we seek is heart-transforming truth that leads to Christlike character and to lives that honor and please God. The Holy Spirit is the one who brings this to the believer.

> The natural person does not accept the things of the Spirit of God, for they are folly to him, and he is not able to understand them because they are spiritually discerned. The spiritual person judges all things, but is himself to be judged by no one. "For who has understood the mind of the Lord so as to instruct him?" But we have the mind of Christ. (1 Cor. 2:14–16)

The illumining work of the Holy Spirit is the indispensable factor in knowing truth that leads to a growing life in Christ. Therefore, as we go to God's Word, we need prayers such as: "Open my eyes, that I may behold wondrous things out of your law" (Ps. 119:18) and

> I do not cease to give thanks for you, remembering you in my prayers, that the God of our Lord Jesus Christ, the Father of glory, may give you the spirit of wisdom and of revelation in the knowledge of him, having the eyes of your hearts enlightened, that you may know what is the hope to which he has called you,

what are the riches of his glorious inheritance in the saints. (Eph. 1:16–18)

(4) We should study the Bible with *eager expectation to learn much* but also expecting to find *great mystery and challenges to our thinking*. God has given us his Word so that we may know him as he is and that the Bible is completely sufficient to lead us to accurate, personal, and sufficient knowledge. But it cannot lead us beyond our finite minds. We will always be limited in our understanding of our infinite God. We should learn to love and celebrate the times when the magnitude of God comes home to us and we find ourselves running out of the intellectual ability to understand all that he is. This tension is discussed in more detail in chapter 3, where we talk about the tension between God being both knowable and incomprehensible at the same time.

(5) We should study the Bible with *humble obedience*. As we learn about God in his Word, the most obvious responses are worship, trust, and obedience. There is no more foundational way to express our trust in God then to obey his commandments. And there is no more fundamental way to express our delight in God than to trust him enough to walk in his ways. Those who earnestly and honestly seek to know God through his Word will quite naturally respond with submission to his Word. God is not pleased with people who are merely playing intellectual games with him, seeking to understand his Word with no intention of trusting and obeying him. The Word of God proves itself true when we put it into action in the obedience of faith. As Jesus says in John 7:17, "If anyone's will is to do God's will, he will know whether the teaching is from God or whether I am speaking on my own authority." The Bible validates its truthfulness when we do what it says.

(6) We should study the Bible with *heartfelt gratitude and joy*. We should never take God's Word for granted. It is a great blessing that God has revealed himself and that we have access to that revelation and Bibles in our own language. There are still thousands of

people groups who do not have translations of the Bible in their native tongue. One of the greatest experiences of our lives was when my wife and I (Erik) attended a dedication ceremony for a Wanca Quechua translation of the New Testament in Peru. People at the ceremony were weeping because they were able to read a Bible in their own language for the first time. I was humbled by their deep appreciation of the Bible and have never looked at my Bible in the same way again.

How amazing that God has revealed himself and that we have that revelation in our own languages on our shelves and on our phones! On top of that, it is a tremendous privilege to be a student who is blessed with the time and resources to devote to knowing God's Word in depth. God treats us as friends when he reveals his Word to us (John 15:15). He lets us in on what he thinks about the most important things. What a fantastic privilege it is to be a friend of Jesus and to be able to learn those things that Jesus himself has learned from the Father. As we learn, we should grow in a deep sense of gratitude for being saved by his grace and for the privilege of being able to study his Word.

Our response to the study of theology from Scripture should be that of the psalmist: "How precious to me are your thoughts, O God!" (Ps. 139:17). Consider these other verses as we conclude our initial thoughts about the study of the Bible and theology:

> The law of the LORD is perfect,
>   reviving the soul;
> the testimony of the LORD is sure,
>   making wise the simple;
> the precepts of the LORD are right,
>   rejoicing the heart;
> the commandment of the LORD is pure. . . .
> More to be desired are they than gold,
>   even much fine gold;
> sweeter also than honey
>   and drippings of the honeycomb.

Moreover, by them is your servant warned;
  in keeping them there is great reward (Ps. 19:7–8, 10–11).

In the way of your testimonies I delight
  as much as in all riches . . .

How sweet are your words to my taste,
  sweeter than honey to my mouth!
Through your precepts I get understanding;
  therefore I hate every false way.

Your word is a lamp to my feet
  and a light to my path. (Ps. 119:14, 103–105)

A CHRISTIAN APPROACH TO BIBLICAL AND THEOLOGICAL STUDIES: ASSUMPTIONS OR PRESUPPOSITIONS AS "FUNCTIONAL ABSOLUTES"

As evangelicals, we do not pretend to study the Bible without presuppositions.[4] We consciously, intentionally, and unapologetically seek to be informed and motivated by explicitly biblical thinking as we study the Bible. Belief in God is foundational for all of life and should guide the way we understand the quest for truth. The Bible tells us that God exists and what he is like, how he has revealed himself, and how we are to relate to him as creatures made in his image. This understanding then determines the method, attitude, and purposes of biblical and theological studies. The God we find in the Bible determines how we approach the Bible. The way we study the Bible is based in certain functional absolutes about God. The following are some of those absolutes.

GOD EXISTS AND HAS REVEALED HIMSELF

The question of God's existence seems like a logical place to start one's process of knowing God. So, you might think that the Bible

---

[4] Much of the rest of this chapter has been adapted from Erik Thoennes, *Life's Biggest Questions: What the Bible Says about the Things That Matter Most* (Wheaton, IL: Crossway, 2011), 41–47, 51–55; and Erik Thoennes, "Biblical Doctrine: An Overview," in The ESV Study Bible®, ESV Bible® (Wheaton, IL: Crossway, 2008), 2505–29.

starts here and makes it a major priority to argue for God's existence, but it doesn't. Rather, it assumes God's existence from the first verse to the last. It also assumes that God has revealed himself in such obvious ways in creation and human experience (Rom. 1:19–21) that to deny his existence would be foolish (Ps. 14:1). The Bible tells us that because of God's personal nature, he must reveal himself if we are to know him personally. God has revealed himself to us in two ways: through special revelation and general revelation.

SPECIAL REVELATION

The Bible is God's written revelation of who he is and what he has done in redemptive history. Humans need this divine, transcendent perspective in order to break out of their subjective, culturally bound, fallen limitations. Through God's written Word, his people may overcome error, grow in sanctification, minister effectively to others, and enjoy abundant lives as God intends.

GENERAL REVELATION

God gives general revelation to all people at all times. This revelation is found both in the external creation ("The heavens declare the glory of God," Ps. 19:1) and in internal human experience ("What can be known about God is plain to them, because God has shown it to them. For his invisible attributes, namely, his eternal power and divine nature, have been clearly perceived, ever since the creation of the world, in the things that have been made. So they are without excuse," Rom. 1:19–20). General revelation shows several of God's attributes, such as his existence, power, creativity, and wisdom; in addition, the testimony of human conscience also provides some evidence of God's moral standards to all human beings (Rom. 2:14–15).

Therefore, from general revelation all people have *some* knowledge that God exists, *some* knowledge of his character, and *some* knowledge of his moral standards. This results in an awareness of guilt before God, as people instinctively know that they have not lived up to his moral requirements. Thus, in the many false religions that have been invented, people attempt to assuage their sense of guilt. But general revelation does not disclose the only true solution to man's guilt before God: the forgiveness of sins that comes through Jesus Christ. This means that general revelation does not provide personal knowledge of God as a loving Father who redeems his people and establishes a covenant with them. For this, one needs *special revelation*, which God has provided in his historical supernatural activities, in the Bible, and definitively in Jesus Christ.

In the quest to know God, it is vital to understand just what it means to really know him. Methods, expectations, and attitudes in studying theology are determined by one's definition of "knowing God." Central to understanding this is the fact that God is both incomprehensible and knowable.

THE INCOMPREHENSIBILITY OF GOD

Scripture teaches that we can have a true and personal knowledge of God, but this does not mean we will ever understand him exhaustively. The Bible is clear that God is ultimately *incomprehensible to us*; that is, we can never fully comprehend his whole being.

> Great is the LORD, and greatly to be praised,
>   and his greatness is unsearchable. (Ps. 145:3)

> Behold, these are but the outskirts of his ways,
>   and how small a whisper do we hear of him!
>   But the thunder of his power who can understand?
>   (Job 26:14)

> For my thoughts are not your thoughts,
>   neither are your ways my ways, declares the LORD.

For as the heavens are higher than the earth,
    so are my ways higher than your ways
    and my thoughts than your thoughts. (Isa. 55:8–9)

Oh, the depth of the riches and wisdom and knowledge of God! How unsearchable are his judgments and how inscrutable his ways!

"For who has known the mind of the Lord,
    or who has been his counselor?" (Rom. 11:33–34)

These verses teach that not only is God's whole being incomprehensible but each of his attributes—his greatness, power, thoughts, ways, wisdom, and judgments—are well beyond human ability to fathom fully. Not only can we never know everything there is to know about God, we can never know everything there is to know about even one aspect of God's character or work.

The main reasons for God's incomprehensibility are: (1) *God is infinite and his creatures are finite.* It is part of the definition of a creature to depend on its Creator for its very existence, and it is therefore limited in all its aspects. Yet God is without limitations in every quality he possesses. This Creator-creature, infinite-finite gap will always exist. (2) *The perfect unity of all God's attributes* is far beyond the realm of human experience. God's love, wrath, grace, justice, holiness, patience, and jealousy are continually functioning in a perfectly integrated yet infinitely complex way. He is also everywhere present and fully aware of all that is happening at every moment, and wisely responding and reacting to all these events. A finite creature cannot comprehend God's perfect, unified response to even two concurrent events. To imagine that God is simultaneously and perfectly aware of, and responding to, all of the murders, weddings, adultery, conversions, births, deaths, acts of kindness and cruelty, will overwhelm even the most brilliant human mind. (3) *The effects of sin* on the minds of fallen humans also greatly inhibit the ability to know God. The tendency of fallen creatures is to distort, pervert, and confuse truth and to use, or rather abuse, it for selfish ends rather than for God's glory (Rom. 1:18–26). (4) A final reason God can never be fully known is that in his sovereign wisdom, *God has chosen not to reveal some things*: "The secret things belong to the LORD our God, but the things that are revealed belong to us and to our children forever, that we may do all the words of this law" (Deut. 29:29). Many would label it unloving for God to decide to withhold some information from his people. They wrongly believe that God should reveal everything they may want to know. Yet as with all good fathers, God's wisdom leads him to refrain from answering all the questions his children ask him, and this contributes to his incomprehensibility.

In heaven, God's incomprehensibility will no doubt be lessened when the effects of sin no longer ravage minds and when he will most likely share some of his secrets. However, God will always be infinite and humans will always be finite, so he will always be beyond human ability to know exhaustively. Because God can never be fully known, those who seek to know God should be deeply humbled in the process, realizing that they will always have more to learn. The appropriate response to God is a heart of wonder and awe in light of his incomprehensible greatness. Christians should do all they can to cultivate hearts of wonder for the awesome God they worship. God's incomprehensibility also means that beliefs can be held with firm conviction even though they may be filled with inexplicable mystery. The Trinity, the divine and human natures of Christ, divine sovereignty and human responsibility, and many other core teachings of the Christian faith are profoundly mysterious; believing them requires a robust affirmation of the incomprehensibility of God.

THE KNOWABILITY OF GOD

The incomprehensibility of God could lead to despair or apathy in the quest to know God, but the Bible also teaches that God is knowable. While God can never be exhaustively understood, he can be known truly, personally, and sufficiently. God is personal, has definite characteristics, and has personally revealed himself so that he can be truly known. The multiplication of grace and peace in our lives is dependent on knowing God, and this knowledge provides sufficient resources for life and for becoming the people God wants us to be.

Knowledge of God in Christ should be our greatest desire and aspiration. It is the basis of attaining eternal life; it is at the heart of life in the new covenant; it was Paul's primary goal; and it leads to godly love. God will never be known absolutely, but we can know things about him that are absolutely true, so much so that we can be willing to live and die for those beliefs. God has provided knowledge of himself that is personal, relational, and sufficient for fruitful, faithful, godly living. No one will ever be able to say he or she lacked the necessary revelation to know God and to start living as God intends.

God's personal and sufficient revelation of himself should foster solid conviction among believers. We need not live in ambiguity and uncertainty about who God is and what he demands of his creatures. The increasing influence of Eastern religions on the West, certain postmodern views of truth, and religious pluralism all emphasize God's incomprehensibility so much that he is eventually made to seem unknowable. It then becomes impossible to say anything definitively true or false about him, and people then think that the only heresy is claiming that there is any heresy at all! On the contrary, because of his gracious revelation and illumination, God can indeed be known. God's knowability should lead to eager, diligent, devoted study of God's Word so that we can understand him as he has revealed himself and avoid any false view of God that will dishonor him. We should never grow apathetic in seeking to know God, because we are in fact able and equipped to know him and to please him with our lives.

TRANSCENDENCE AND IMMANENCE

God is both transcendent (majestic and holy, far greater than his creatures) and immanent (near and present, fully involved with his creatures). To understand the God of the Bible, this vital biblical balance must be appreciated. God is distinct from and far above all he has made: "The LORD is high above all nations, and his glory above the heavens! Who is like the LORD our God, who is seated on high, who looks far down on the heavens and the earth?" (Ps. 113:4–6). Yet he is also always actively, personally engaged with his creation: "Yet he is actually not far from each one of us, for 'In him we live and move and have our being'; as even some of your own poets have said, 'For we are indeed his offspring'" (Acts 17:27–28). Those most humbled by God's majesty and holiness most experience personal closeness with him: "For thus says the One who is high and lifted up, who inhabits eternity, whose name is Holy: 'I dwell in the high and holy place [transcendence], and also with him who is of a contrite and lowly spirit, to revive the spirit of the lowly, and to revive the heart of the contrite [immanence]'" (Isa. 57:15).

Non-Christian religions tend toward one extreme or the other—either to a god who is so "other than" creation that nothing meaningful can be said about him (e.g., Eastern and New Age religions), or to one who is so "identified with" creation that his majestic holiness is lost (e.g., Greco-Roman and much current Western religion). An accurate understanding of God deeply appreciates both his awesome otherness and his intimate nearness. Christians relate to a God who is both the great "I AM" and "the God of your fathers" (Ex. 3:14–15). He is the eternal, infinite God who has stepped not only into time and space but also into covenant relationship with his people through the incarnation of Christ. The biblical balance between God's transcendence and his immanence is hard to maintain, but the best worship, prayer, and daily relating to God is that which has in it a deep recognition of both God's majestic holiness and his personal engagement with the creatures he has made.

FUNCTIONAL ABSOLUTES REGARDING SCRIPTURE
THE INSPIRATION OF SCRIPTURE

The Bible is God-breathed (see 2 Tim. 3:16) and gets its true, authoritative, powerful, holy character from God himself, who inspired human authors to write exactly what he wanted them to write. Instead of merely dictating words to them, God worked through their unique personalities and circumstances. Scripture is therefore both fully human and fully divine. It is both the testimony of men to God's revelation, and divine revelation itself. "No prophecy of Scripture comes from someone's own interpretation. For no prophecy was ever produced by the will of man, but men spoke from God as they were carried along by the Holy Spirit" (2 Pet. 1:20–21). Because the Bible is God's Word in human words, it can be trusted as the definitive revelation from the mouth of God himself.

THE INERRANCY OF SCRIPTURE

The doctrine of inerrancy means that the Bible is entirely truthful and reliable in all that it affirms in its original manuscripts. Another way of saying this is that the Bible does not affirm anything that is contrary to fact. Because God is the ultimate author of the Bible, and because God is always perfectly truthful, it follows that his Word is completely truthful as well: he is the "God who never lies" (Titus 1:2). It would be contrary to his character to affirm anything false. God is all knowing, always truthful and good, and all powerful, so he always knows and tells the truth and is able to communicate and preserve his Word. "O Lord God, you are God, and *your words are true*, and you have promised this good thing to your servant" (2 Sam. 7:28). "Every word of God proves true" (Prov. 30:5; see Ps. 12:6; 119:42; John 17:17). Inerrancy does not require twenty-first-century precision or scientifically technical language. The following quotation from the *Chicago Statement on Biblical Inerrancy* summarizes what inerrancy does *not* mean:

> We affirm the propriety of using inerrancy as a theological term
> with reference to the complete truthfulness of Scripture. We deny
> that it is proper to evaluate Scripture according to standards of
> truth and error that are alien to its usage or purpose. We further
> deny that inerrancy is negated by Biblical phenomena such as a
> lack of modern technical precision, irregularities of grammar or
> spelling, observational descriptions of nature, the reporting of
> falsehoods, the use of hyperbole and round numbers, the topical
> arrangement of material, variant selections of material in paral-
> lel accounts, or the use of free citations.[5]

The inerrancy of Scripture gives the believer great confidence
in the Bible as his sure foundation for understanding all that God
wants him to know and all that the believer needs for godliness
and eternal life.

THE CLARITY OF SCRIPTURE

The Bible itself acknowledges that some passages of Scripture are
"hard to understand" (2 Pet. 3:16, referring to some aspects of
Paul's letters). In general, however, with the illumination of the
Spirit (2 Tim. 2:7), the Bible is clear to all who seek understanding
with the goal of knowing and obeying God.

Old Testament believers were instructed to teach God's commands continually to their children with the expectation that they
would understand it: "These words that I command you today shall
be on your heart. You shall teach them diligently to your children,
and shall talk of them when you sit in your house, and when you
walk by the way, and when you lie down, and when you rise" (Deut.
6:6–7). God's Word is said to "[make] wise the simple" (Ps. 19:7).
Jesus based his teaching squarely on the Old Testament Scriptures:
he assumed its teaching was clear and would often ask, "Have you
not read . . . ?" (see Matt. 12:3, 5; 19:4; 21:42; 22:31).

Because of the basic clarity of the Bible, when Christians

---

[5] *Chicago Statement on Biblical Inerrancy*, art. 8.

disagree over the meaning of a passage, they can assume that the problem is not with the Bible but rather with themselves as interpreters. Misunderstandings may be due to various factors such as human sin, ignorance of enough of the relevant data, faulty assumptions, or trying to reach a definite conclusion about a topic for which the Bible has not given enough information to decide the question. The Bible is mostly clear, and ordinary believers are capable of comprehending Scripture for themselves. In addition, God provides teachers of his Word to further help his people's understanding (1 Cor. 12:28; Eph. 4:11). Believers have the responsibility to read, interpret, and understand the Bible because it is basically clear. This was an assumption of the Protestant Reformers who sought to translate the Bible into the language of the common people. They believed that all true Christians are priests who are able to know God through his Word and to help others do the same.

THE SUFFICIENCY OF SCRIPTURE

Scripture provides all the words from God that we need in order to know God truly and personally and to live abundant, godly lives (Ps. 19:7–9; 2 Tim. 3:15). God has given his people a sufficient revelation of himself so that they are able to know, trust, and obey him. "All Scripture is breathed out by God and profitable for teaching, for reproof, for correction, and for training in righteousness, that the man of God may be complete, equipped for every good work" (2 Tim. 3:16–17).

God commands that nothing be added or taken away from the Bible, which indicates that it has always been exactly what he has wanted at each stage in its development throughout the history of salvation. "You shall not add to the word that I command you, nor take from it, that you may keep the commandments of the LORD your God that I command you" (Deut. 4:2; see Deut. 12:32; Prov. 30:5–6). The powerful admonition against tampering (with God's Word) that stands at the conclusion of the entire Bible applies primarily, of course, to the book of Revelation, but in a secondary sense, what it says may be applied to the Bible as a whole: "I warn everyone who hears the words of the prophecy of this book: if anyone adds to them, God will add to him the plagues described in this book, and if anyone takes away from the words of the book of this prophecy, God will take away his share in the tree of life and in the holy city, which are described in this book" (Rev. 22:18–19).

Believers should find freedom and encouragement in the knowledge that God has provided all of the absolutely authoritative instruction that they need in order to know him and live as he intends. God's people should never fear that he has withheld something they might need him to say in order for them to know how to please him, or that he will have to somehow supplement his Word with new instructions for some new situation that arises in the modern age. (The New Testament allows for the activity of the Holy Spirit in leading and guiding individuals, as in Rom. 8:14; Gal. 5:16, 18, 25; but this guidance is always in line with Scripture, never in opposition to scriptural commands.) Therefore believers should be satisfied with what Scripture teaches and what it leaves unsaid. "The secret things belong to the LORD our God, but the things that are revealed belong to us and to our children forever, that we may do all the words of this law" (Deut. 29:29).

JESUS'S VIEW OF THE BIBLE

The most convincing reason to believe that the Bible is inspired, inerrant, clear, and sufficient is because this is what Jesus believed. His teaching assumed that the Old Testament was the authoritative Word of his Father: "Do not think that I have come to abolish the Law or the Prophets; I have not come to abolish them but to fulfill them. For truly, I say to you, until heaven and earth pass away, not an iota, not a dot, will pass from the Law until all is accomplished" (Matt. 5:17–18). Jesus referred to dozens of Old Testament persons and events and always treated Old Testament history as historically accurate. He quoted from Genesis as his Father's Word when he said,

> Have you not read that he who created them from the beginning made them male and female, and said, 'Therefore a man shall leave his father and his mother and hold fast to his wife, and the two shall become one flesh'? So they are no longer two but one flesh. What therefore God has joined together, let not man separate. (Matt. 19:4–6)

Jesus not only assumed that the creation story was true, he also freely quoted words from the Old Testament narrator as words that God himself "said." It is not uncommon for Jesus's theological arguments to depend on the truthfulness of the Old Testament account (Matt. 5:12; 11:23–24; 12:41–42; 24:37–39; Luke 4:25–27; 11:50–51; John 8:56–58). Jesus's view of the Old Testament as the Word of God aligns with the way the Old Testament regularly speaks of itself.

Jesus saw his entire life as a fulfillment of Scripture (Matt. 26:54; Mark 8:31). Throughout his life, Jesus used Scripture to resist temptation (Matt. 4:1–11) and to settle disputes (Matt. 19:1–12; 22:39; Mark 7:1–13; Luke 10:25–26). Jesus died quoting Scripture (cf. Matt. 27:46 with Ps. 22:1). On his resurrection day, he explained Scripture at length on the Emmaus road and to his disciples in Jerusalem (Luke 24:13–17, 44–47). Conscious of his identity as God the Son, Jesus saw his teaching as no less divinely inspired than the Old Testament. Jesus taught with an authority that distinguished him from other teachers of the law. He interpreted the law on his own authority rather than depending on rabbinic sources (Matt. 5:21–48). He described his teaching and the law as sharing the same permanence: "Heaven and earth will pass away, but my words will not pass away" (Matt. 24:35; cf. Matt. 5:17–18; John 14:10, 24). Jesus viewed both the Old Testament and his own teaching as the Word of God. The New Testament apostolic witness was a result of Jesus giving his disciples authority and power through the Holy Spirit to impart spiritual truths in writing no less than by word of mouth (Mark 3:13–19; John 16:12–14; Acts 26:16–18; 1 Cor. 2:12–13). Jesus took Scripture to be the authoritative Word of God upon which he based his entire life. Those who follow Christ are called to treat Scripture (Old Testament and New Testament together) in the same way. For Christians, the Bible is a source of great delight and joy and God is to be diligently sought in his Word (1 Pet. 2:2). The Word of God is a precious treasure that deserves to be studied, meditated upon, and obeyed.

CONCLUSION

God has spoken. He created us for himself and speaks to us so our relationship with him is truthful and life giving. God's Word has the power to change our hearts and bring us out of death and darkness. The Word of God gives us the capacity to love him with all our hearts as well as with all our minds (Matt. 22:37). The response of our hearts should be one of great joy and delight in God and the truths of his Word.

Studying the Bible requires hard work, discipline, humility, and the commitment to working it out in daily life, it also gives us the basis of faith, hope, and love. Biblical teaching is the well from which we draw persevering faith in times of great trial and humble gratitude in times of victory. Study of the Bible equips us to fulfill our primary purpose, which is to glorify and delight in God through deep personal knowledge of him.

Over the combined half-century, we (Wilkins and Thoennes) have been teaching biblical studies and theology in university and church contexts, we have seen that when the truths of the

Bible are faithfully taught and humbly applied, this consistently leads to the Spirit's transforming work in the lives of his people. Christlike character, courage, love, faith, perseverance, and the fruit of the Spirit have always flourished as God works through transformed thinking according to his Word.[6]

---

[6] For very helpful resources on the relationship between the intellectual and spiritual life of students of the Bible, see: Kelly Kapic, *A Little Book for New Theologians: Why and How to Study Theology* (Downers Grove, IL: IVP Academic, 2012); John Frame, "Studying Theology as a Servant of Jesus," Frame-Poythress.org, June 5, 2012, http://frame-poythress.org/studying-theology-as-a-servant-of -jesus/; Joanne Jung, *Knowing Grace: Cultivating a Lifestyle of Godliness* (Downers Grove IL: Inter-Varsity Press, 2011); John Piper, "The Supremacy of God in the Life of the Mind" (address, Northwest College Chapel, February 16, 1993), https://www.desiringgod.org/messages/the-supremacy-of -god-in-the-life-of-the-mind; Walt Russell, *Playing with Fire: How the Bible Ignites Change in Your Soul* (Colorado Springs: NavPress, 2000); Benjamin B. Warfield, "The Religious Life of Theological Students," *TMSJ* 6, no. 2 (Fall 1995): 181–95.

2

BIBLICAL STUDIES

Biblical studies by its very title is the study of the Bible, but as an academic discipline, it is a collection of various sub-disciplines that cluster to make up the whole. There is a wide spectrum of these sub-disciplines (e.g., from Egyptology and Assyriology, to linguistics and sociology, to literary theory and ethics), but here we focus on the primary approaches.[1]

SUB-DISCIPLINES OF BIBLICAL STUDIES

1. HERMENUTICS

The science and art of "hermeneutics" attempts to establish methodological principles of interpretation, especially of written texts. "Biblical hermeneutics" concentrates on principles of interpretation of the Bible and has special relevance as a sub-discipline of biblical studies. Two important approaches to hermeneutics stand out as important for those beginning biblical studies.

In the first place, developing a consistent hermeneutical method is the responsibility of all Christians, and is one of the first courses we should take in the academic study of the Bible. Whether or not we have had a formal course in hermeneutics, all of us interpret the Bible in all of our readings, in the same way that all of us have learned to interpret various forms of communication from our earliest years. "Sunrise" and "sunset" are common expressions in everyday spoken and written life, but we had to learn

---

[1] For an overview and in-depth analysis of the various sub-disciplines, see J. W. Rogerson and Judith M. Lieu, eds., *The Oxford Handbook of Biblical Studies* (Oxford: Oxford University Press, 2006).

as children that the sun doesn't actually "rise" or "set." We all now know that they are "phenomenological expressions" used to describe the way the sun appears to act as the earth rotates. One day in class, a professor referred to his daughter as a "gnarly athlete." The professor intended to communicate that his daughter, who had just completed running 52.4 miles in an ultramarathon, was beyond radical and beyond extreme as an athlete, and he meant it in an enormously positive way. However, some international students had only heard the term *gnarly* used in a negative way to describe a person who was contorted physically. Miscommunication and misinterpretation resulted that had to be clarified. That is the application of basic hermeneutics to spoken and written language in everyday life.

In like fashion, we have learned from earliest years to interpret the Bible. Jesus made the following well-known statement: "I am the door. If anyone enters by me, he will be saved and will go in and out and find pasture" (John 10:9). We recognize intuitively that Jesus does not have hinges on his arms and legs or a doorknob on his forehead. We recognize that when we are saved, we do not find a pasture so that we can graze like cattle. By long association with the verse, we recognize that Jesus is not a *literal* door to a house but is using "metaphorical language" to speak of himself as the entrance to the secure, peaceful life of salvation. From our earliest days as Christians, we learn basic principles for interpreting the Bible so that we can hear God's message through human written language.

As we deepen our study of the Bible, we need further training in our methods of interpreting the Bible. For example, the apostle Paul culminates an important discussion of the unity that believers have in Christ with the statement: "There is neither Jew nor Greek, there is neither slave nor free, there is no male and female, for you are all one in Christ Jesus" (Gal. 3:28). On one level we understand immediately that Paul is referring to the barriers between humans that are broken down in Christ, but this verse needs further examination hermeneutically. Is this to be taken literally or figuratively? Is this theological only, or does this refer to political orientation or gender references? This verse has been interpreted in many different ways, and often basic hermeneutical rules are ignored. We all need a solid hermeneutical foundation that deepens as our study of the Bible deepens.[2]

One of the beginning tools of biblical studies in a Christian school of higher education is learning the practice of wise interpretation of the literary forms, figures of speech, and genres of the Bible. This means to read the biblical text in the way that the biblical authors intended them to be read.[3] The course may be called "Bible Study Methods" or "Biblical Interpretation" or "Introduction to Bible Study and Interpretation," all of which are intended to teach the basics of biblical hermeneutics. The apostle Paul gave a stirring guideline to his companion Timothy that has relevance for us as we attempt to interpret the Bible: "Do your best to present yourself to God as one approved, a worker who has no need to be ashamed, rightly handling the word of truth" (2 Tim. 2:15). In the Bible we handle the truth from God in human language, and we need to do so responsibly.

Secondly, hermeneutics is a sub-discipline of biblical studies for those involved in advanced studies and specialization. Hermeneutics is often engaged as a subset of philosophy, where students are occupied with the theoretical questions related to the possibility of determining the meaning of human language and communicative acts. That has been a profound area of specialization in modern biblical studies, especially from the challenges of postmodern literary theory that on many levels questioned the

---

[2] See Walter C. Kaiser Jr. and Moisés Silva, "Who Needs Hermeneutics Anyway?" in *An Introduction to Biblical Hermeneutics: The Search for Meaning* (Grand Rapids, MI: Zondervan, 1994), 14–25.

[3] A good starting point is Walt Russell, *Playing with Fire: How the Bible Ignites Change in Your Soul* (Colorado Springs: NavPress, 2000), which blends beginning hermeneutics with intentional spiritual formation in the life of the Christian reader.

possibility of knowing the meaning of a communicative act. This is a burgeoning new field of study, as it blends philosophical epistemology, literary theory, and exegesis in the quest for a theological reading of Scripture.[4]

2. OLD TESTAMENT AND NEW TESTAMENT STUDIES

For Christians, the sixty-six books of the Bible are divided into two basic sections, which are commonly known as the thirty-nine books of the Old Testament and the twenty-seven books of the New Testament. The Greek term for "covenant" (*diatheke*) was used to refer to the old covenant God had made with Israel, which served as a foundation for the new covenant in Jesus. The term "covenant" was translated "*testamentum*" by the Latin Bible, the Vulgate, and was subsequently used by Christians to refer to the Old and New Testaments. Some undergraduate colleges and universities offer a combined introductory course called "The Bible." Others offer two separate courses, one on the Old Testament (sometimes called "the Hebrew Bible") and another on the New Testament (sometimes called "the Christian Scriptures"). It is preferable to take courses that cover the whole Bible, since for Christians the Old and New Testament together comprise the Bible.

Although the Bible as a whole has events that transpired over a span of thousands of years and in several different cultural settings, several cords unite both Old and New Testament. One is their divine authorship. All of the books of the Bible are recognized by Christians to be God's Word. The apostle Paul states emphatically, "For whatever was written in former days was written for our instruction, that through endurance and through the encouragement of the Scriptures we might have hope" (Rom. 15:4).

Another cord is that the Old Testament is foundational for understanding the New Testament. The Genesis accounts of the

---

[4]For a good overview of this sub-discipline, see Andreas J. Köstenberger and Richard D. Patterson, *Invitation to Biblical Interpretation: Exploring the Hermeneutical Triad of History, Literature, and Theology*, Invitation to Theological Studies series (Grand Rapids, MI: Kregel, 2011), 57–86.

creation of the earth, the creation of humans to rule for God, and the fall of Adam and Eve and the entrance of sin in this world lay the foundation for the New Testament understanding of humans created in the image of God (1 Cor. 15:49), the new creation (Rom. 8:19–23; 2 Cor. 5:17), and the kingdom of God on earth (1 Thess. 2:12).

Similarly, New Testament authors consistently look back to the Old Testament promises and prophecies and see that their fulfillment is found in events of the New Testament era. This is especially the case with the person and work of Jesus Christ on earth, which is the climax of history. His birth and early ministry fulfilled the promise of a virgin-born Savior (cf. Isa. 7:14; Matt. 1:20–25); his crucifixion, death, resurrection, and ascension fulfilled the hope lodged in the sacrificial system (cf. Leviticus 4; Hebrews 10); and redemption through his blood fulfilled God's most central purposes in his history of salvation (cf. Isa. 9:6–7; Gal. 4:4–5).

Old Testament studies. But Old Testament studies is a special focus of study in itself. On the most basic level, it aims to acquaint students with the life, customs, and thought of the Hebrew people and their neighbors in the biblical and related periods. It studies the literary genre, structure, and themes of each book and the purpose of the writers, and studies selected introductory and critical issues (e.g., authorship, dating, setting) and crucial problems (e.g., prophecy). On a more advanced level, students are given instruction in the original languages with an accurate foundation in Hebrew and Aramaic grammar, syntax, and exegesis, so that their expositions of the English translations will reflect a sound basis of interpretation.

New Testament studies. New Testament studies are also a special focus of study. The Christian revelation recorded in the New Testament has served as the lens through which much of the Western world had understood the whole Word of God. The Jesus Christ of the New Testament is the central axis of all of history, and an encounter with him is found in the truthful revelation of the New Testament. Jews, Muslims, and Christians are referred to by Muslims as "People of the Book," because all three faiths are constituted by a revelation of the will of God rooted in the Old Testament. But New Testament Christianity is unique, precisely because of the person and work of Jesus Christ. Mark Henrie states emphatically,

> While Jews and Muslims revere their scriptures as the Word of God delivered by patriarchs and prophets, for Christians, Christ was himself "the Word [of God] made flesh." Christ does not *write*; he *is* and he *acts*. Still, for nearly twenty centuries the men and women of the west have found the meaning of their collective and personal existence revealed in the text of the Christian Bible, and no liberal education is complete without an encounter with that Word.[5]

The mission of New Testament studies is to help students develop skills in the areas of interpretation of the books of the New Testament, the historical-cultural setting, and biblical theology. The intended outcome is for students to better understand God's written Word in order to apply it to the development of a distinctly Christian worldview that they would live out in daily life and ministries in the presence of the living Word of God.[6]

3. HISTORICAL ANALYSIS

Historical analysis is of vital importance in understanding the Bible because the authors record what actually took place in space and time. They did not make up their stories in order to have a nice, packaged religion that supported their doctrinal presuppositions. They were either witnesses or recorders or prophets of

---

[5] Mark C. Henrie, *A Student's Guide to the Core Curriculum* (Wilmington, DE: Intercollegiate Studies Institute, 2000), 47.
[6] This summary is drawn in part from *Biola University Catalog 2015–16* (Biola University, 2015), 59–60.

the heart of the message that God had acted in history. Moses, David, Jeremiah, Peter, and Paul were historical figures who were impacted by God's activity in history, and they wrote to record that activity. And preeminently, Jesus was not some ghostlike apparition, less than a true human being; the authors of the Gospels were motivated by the fact that they were, as Ralph Martin states, "reporting solid history, and that the chief actor in their drama was a flesh-and-blood character, living a human life under Palestinian skies."[7] This historical record was the basis of the biblical authors' faith.

Therefore, the goal of historical analysis of the Old Testament is the historical and cultural examination of a period in Israel's history (exodus and conquest, judges, united monarchy, divided monarchy, Judah to the fall of Jerusalem, post-exilic), using available biblical and extra-biblical materials. Extra-biblical materials include archaeology (which is the history of excavation), history, and geography of the land and their bearings upon the Old Testament. Also, studies of the Qumran community and Dead Sea Scrolls, its belief and practices, and the relationship of the findings to Old and New Testament studies are important extra-biblical materials.

Similarly, the goal of historical analysis in the New Testament is to examine historical backgrounds and archaeology, including a study of the religious developments, literature, geography, and cultural setting of Judaism and the Hellenistic world at the time of Christ and the early church. This also includes an examination of such things as Jewish religious beliefs and customs, the political situation, urban life, folk belief, ethnic issues, language, Greco-Roman religious beliefs and customs, and other cultural phenomena that form the relevant background to the New Testament.

---

[7] Ralph P. Martin, *New Testament Foundations: A Guide for Students, Volume 1: The Four Gospels* (Grand Rapids, MI: Eerdmans, 1975), 43.

4. LITERARY ANALYSIS

The Bible is not only a historical record of God's activities in history, but is recorded as literature, which requires literary analysis. This may seem like an unnecessary element to include, since the Bible is obviously a literary document. But, it is important to keep in mind that the Bible is literature, and the authors took great lengths to compose documents that would communicate to their audiences. Therefore, we benefit immensely by examining elements of literary design and structure in each book of the Bible, and each will vary according to the author's particular purposes, genre, style, and audience. For example, the analysis of the Psalms of the Old Testament will include the nature, scope, and principles of Hebrew poetry in comparison with the poetry of other cultures of the ancient Near East. And the study of the Psalms should include historical and theological reflections, but also place particular emphasis upon their devotional and practical values as the reader is drawn into the author's own life lived with God. Likewise, application of literary analysis to the prophecies of the book of Revelation involves a discussion not only of crucial background and critical issues but also the book's literary structure and purposes, which, when understood, will help overcome interpretive difficulties and lead to practical implications of the book for the reader.

5. THEOLOGICAL ANALYSIS

In the discipline of biblical studies, the primary theological analysis is carried out under the banner of biblical theology, which is an intriguing study of the storyline and thematic emphases of Scripture as a whole, and/or limited portions of Scripture. It is the systematic presentation of biblical themes, teachings, and doctrines. Biblical theology has, for many, the basic mission of showing the historical progressiveness of revelation in the Bible, whether that means tracing God's history of salvation,[8] his promise-plan for his people,[9] the establishment of his kingdom on earth,[10] the covenants established with his people,[11] the history of the replication of God's moral and spiritual character (and behavior) in his people,[12] or the discipleship relationship between God and his people.[13] Depending upon one's interest, conviction, or theological persuasion, the study of biblical theology will focus on various time periods, authors, or types of literature. For instance, there is biblical theology of Scripture as a whole, and there is Old Testament theology and New Testament theology. Within the New Testament, there is a theology of the Gospels, Acts, epistles (including Pauline, Petrine, etc.) and apocalypse; within the Gospels, there is the theology of Matthew, Mark, Luke, and John. A Johannine theology addresses a diverse genre of Gospel, epistles, and apocalypse. And carefully grounded biblical theology will in turn lead to a biblical systematic theology, as we will see below.

6. HISTORY OF INTERPRETATION

A very important check on our biblical studies is the history of interpretation. Here, we go outside of the Bible and view the way that the Bible has been interpreted throughout history. The Bible has been studied for thousands of years, so we stand in a long historical stream of interpretation. While our primary concern is to study the Bible itself to find its meaning, we can learn much from others who have gone before us. Past students of the Bible

---

[8] George Eldon Ladd, *A Theology of the New Testament*, ed. Donald A. Hagner, rev. ed. (1974; Grand Rapids, MI: Eerdmans, 1993), 12–28.

[9] Walter C. Kaiser Jr., *The Promise-Plan of God: A Biblical Theology of the Old and New Testaments* (Grand Rapids, MI: Zondervan, 2008), 17–31.

[10] Mark Saucy, *The Kingdom of God in the Teaching of Jesus in 20th Century Theology* (Dallas, TX: Word, 1997), xxi–xl.

[11] Jonathan Lunde, *Following Jesus, The Servant King: A Biblical Theology of Covenantal Theology* (Grand Rapids, MI: Zondervan, 2010), 25–32.

[12] Ben Witherington III, *The Indelible Image: The Theological and Ethical Thought World of the New Testament, Volume One: The Individual Witnesses* (Downers Grove, IL: InterVarsity, 2009), 19–24.

[13] Michael J. Wilkins, *Following the Master: A Biblical Theology of Discipleship* (Grand Rapids, MI: Zondervan, 1992), 17–47.

have influenced us either directly or indirectly, whether or not we are aware of it. We may assume that a particular interpretation is the true meaning of a text, but it may be that we have merely assimilated through sermons, discussions, or readings what others before us have given as an interpretation. There are many strengths and excellent insights that we can gain from others, while there are also many weaknesses and dangerous pitfalls that we can avoid by studying the history of interpretation. Through this kind of study, our growth in understanding the Bible can be facilitated, and we can avoid being sidetracked by rejecting those interpretations that have consistently been found faulty through church history.[14]

CONTEMPORARY ISSUES IN BIBLICAL STUDIES

The biblical studies student has an extensive array of foundational issues, which we have now discussed, that prepare us to interact with significant contemporary issues in biblical studies. We look here at some of the most important issues, which also may offer the most benefit for the beginning student and the believing community.

1. LANGUAGES OF THE BIBLE

A contemporary issue in biblical studies research is the interdisciplinary emphasis of New Testament Greek and linguistics, the scientific study of languages. This integration between two disciplines began in the nineteenth century when scholars took on a philological approach to languages, paying attention to the evolution of languages and classifying them into families.[15] In the twentieth century, linguists in the United States began to approach language in a structural and descriptive way because they

---

[14] For a very fine, brief overview of the history of interpretation of the New Testament from the early church to today, see David S. Dockery, "New Testament Interpretation: A Historical Survey," in *Interpreting the New Testament: Essays on Methods and Issues*, ed. David Alan Black and David S. Dockery (Nashville: B&H, 2001), 21–44. A more extensive study is found in Gerald Bray, *Biblical Interpretation: Past and Present* (Downers Grove, IL: InterVarsity, 1996).

[15] David A. Black, "The Study of New Testament Greek in the Light of Ancient and Modern Linguistics," in *Interpreting the New Testament: Essays on Methods and Issues*, ed. David A. Black and David S. Dockery (Nashville: B&H, 2001), 243.

discovered that "language is a system of interdependent elements rather than a collection of unconnected individual items."[16] James Barr, author of *Semantics of Biblical Language* (1961), critiqued the nonlinguistic approaches to theology and biblical languages and was a part of shifting biblical research methods to integrate with linguistic principles and theory.[17] Scholarship in biblical languages today continues to focus on advancing grammatical study of biblical languages and seeks to apply the tool of linguistics to the process of hermeneutics and exegesis. In *Linguistics and Biblical Interpretation*, Cotterell and Turner turn our attention to this interdisciplinary focus.

> Linguistics may make us more aware of what we are looking for in general—how texts or spoken utterances mean something. It may also open our eyes to features of the way people use language that we had not considered, and to signals of meaning in our text which we had not previously observed, or of which we had not appreciated the significance.[18]

Because God has chosen to communicate inerrant truth through the finite vehicle of human languages, a way to hear and honor the words of Scripture is by paying attention to the nature of language.[19] For this reason, without losing sight of the Bible as divine revelation, we need to view it also as a linguistic artifact.[20]

Material on the grammar for biblical languages is vast, but there are three broad maxims of language that are helpful when one engages with biblical languages in the task of biblical interpretation. First, language, as an instrument of communication, is located in culture, so it is necessary to study original languages

---

[16] Black, "Study of New Testament Greek," 249.

[17] Black, "Study of New Testament Greek," 249.

[18] Peter Cotterell and Max Turner, *Linguistics and Biblical Interpretation* (Downers Grove, IL: InterVarsity, 1989), 32.

[19] Jeannine K. Brown, *Scripture as Communication: Introducing Biblical Hermeneutics* (Grand Rapids, MI: Baker Academic, 2007), 171.

[20] Brown, *Scripture as Communication*, 167.

with the social and cultural settings in which the document was written.[21] By paying attention to the cultural context, one may be able to identify and define words, phrases, and sayings found in the text. For example, the biblical text communicates that Herod is the king of Israel (Matt. 2:1). By reading more about Herod from reliable background resources, one will be informed that Herod was an emissary of Rome, not a Jewish king.[22] This historical insight helps us see Matthew's purpose for including Herod in the birth narratives of Jesus, the true King of the Jews.

Second, communication through language takes place at the utterance level. Communication does not happen at the level of isolated words, but at the level of sentences and discourses.[23] In the mid-twentieth century, it was common among biblical theologians to define theological concepts at the level of an individual word, such as "faith." Barr introduced a linguistic shift for biblical studies: "Theological thought of the type found in the New Testament has its characteristic linguistic expression not in the words individually, but in the word-combination or sentence."[24] Even though meaning is communicated at the utterance level, grammatical and lexical (word) analyses remain important and useful for exegeting the text. Grammatical analysis considers the morphology, the classes and structures of words such as verb tenses. It also considers syntax, which is "the arrangements and interrelationships of words in larger constructions."[25] The study of individual words still plays a role, for words are "the basic blocks for conveying meaning,"[26] but the priority is to understand "how words function together to form a coherent discourse."[27]

---

[21] Brown, *Scripture as Communication*, 177.

[22] Brown, *Scripture as Communication*, 178.

[23] Brown, *Scripture as Communication*, 175.

[24] James Barr, *The Semantics of Biblical Language*, quoted in Brown, *Scripture as Communication*, 175.

[25] Gordon D. Fee, *New Testament Exegesis: A Handbook for Students and Pastors* (Louisville, KY: Westminster John Knox, 2002), 71.

[26] Fee, *New Testament Exegesis*, 79.

[27] Brown, *Scripture as Communication*, 176.

Lastly, the third principle is: "The use of language in utterance communication is highly flexible."[28] Authors may use the same word, but each author has a different sense, which is then determined by the contextual evidence. In James 2:17–20, James's sense of *faith* is the Christian truth. The content of the Christian's faith should lead to works. However, in Romans 4:2–5, Paul's sense of *faith* is more likely trust and belief. Abraham's faith is reckoned as righteousness because he believed God.[29]

2. THE USE OF BACKGROUNDS

The use of backgrounds in biblical interpretation is a cross-cultural experience for every biblical studies student. No biblical text is an island on its own; we can only thoroughly arrive at the meaning of a text by getting behind it,[30] into the historical, cultural, and social world and immediate context of the author. The goal of exploring the background of the Old and New Testament is to capture the theological message of the author and to apply God's Word to our lives in the twenty-first century.

In using background resources, it is helpful to keep the levels of context in mind. "World context" refers to concepts and experiences that are applied universally.[31] "Cultural context" refers to the specific way of living in a particular society.[32] This level covers the political, social, religious customs, and worldview of a given society. Because this level of context includes many areas of study, a realistic approach is to look for domains of study, such as family customs in the Mediterranean world, politics, education, or military and war. For example, the raising of Jairus's daughter from the dead may require us to research a background of mourning in Jewish

---

[28] Brown, *Scripture as Communication*, 178.

[29] Brown, *Scripture as Communication*, 180.

[30] Jon Levenson, *The Hebrew Bible, the Old Testament, and Historical Criticism* (Louisville, KY: Westminster John Knox, 1993), 110–11.

[31] Brown, *Scripture as Communication*, 191. For example, the metaphor of light is understood across many cultures for what is right and true, whereas the metaphor of darkness is typically understood as what is wrong (Ps. 119:105).

[32] Brown, *Scripture as Communication*, 191.

culture. "Audience context" refers to the experience and situation of the text's immediate audience.[33] This involves studying the particular social and political climate of a certain time period, city, or local church. For example, it is crucial to understand the context of Paul's audience when he wrote to local churches in Asia Minor. When we understand the context of the Corinthian congregation, we can better understand Paul's intention in addressing major issues such as eating sacrifices to idols, immorality, and spiritual gifts (1 Corinthians 10–12). By paying attention to these levels of background studies, one may be able to prevent the act of reading one's own cultural assumptions into the text, and interact instead with the thought world of the author, the worldview and circumstances of the immediate audience, and the actual words in the text.

Furthermore, there are two main approaches to background studies: a diachronic approach and a synchronic approach. A *diachronic* approach looks into the chronological events in biblical history. This includes the Old Testament story and Intertestamental history (Second Temple Judaism), which is the period from the end of the Old Testament to the dawn of the New Testament, and the destruction of Jerusalem in AD 70.[34] A diachronic analysis provides the way for a synchronic analysis of the Bible's background, which is a growing area of research among New Testament scholars today.[35] A *synchronic* approach analyzes culture and highlights the manners, customs, institutions, and principles that were relevant to a particular time and environment.[36] The diachronic and

---

[33] Brown, *Scripture as Communication*, 192.

[34] J. Julius Scott, *Jewish Backgrounds of the New Testament* (Grand Rapids, MI: Baker Academic, 1995), 73–106: "Intertestamental History (515 BCE–70 AD): (1) The Jews at the end of the Old Testament (722–586 BCE); (2) The Jews Under the Declining Babylonian Exile (586–539 BCE); (3) The Jews Under Persian Rule (539–331 BCE); (4) The Jews Under Hellenistic Rule (331–143 BCE); (5) The Jews Under Hasmonean Rule (143–63 BCE); (6) The Jews Under Roman Rule (63 BCE–192 CE); (7) The Jews After the Destruction of Jerusalem (70–192 CE)."

[35] Suggested reading for cultural context of the New Testament includes David A. DeSilva, *Honor, Patronage, Kinship, and Purity: Unlocking New Testament Culture* (Downers Grove, IL: InterVarsity, 2000); Bruce W. Longenecker, *The Lost Letters of Pergamum: A Story from the New Testament World* (Grand Rapids, MI: Baker, 2003); and Moyer V. Hubbard, *Christianity in the Greco-Roman World* (Peabody, MA: Hendrickson, 2010).

[36] This applies to the level of cultural and audience context.

synchronic approaches both require the Bible and extra-biblical sources to guide us into the world of the Old Testament, Second Temple Judaism, and the New Testament.

Since the setting of the Old Testament is the Ancient Near East (ANE) world, written records from other ancient people groups in the ANE, such as Egyptians and Mesopotamians, provide background information of the practices and beliefs of Israel's neighboring nations. An area on research is comparison of ANE religious literature to the Pentateuch (Genesis–Deuteronomy) for the purpose of enhancing the interpretation of the Pentateuch. The covenant nature of the Old Testament parallels "the so-called suzerainty covenants in the ancient world, especially those of the Hittites."[37] A suzerain covenant takes place between a powerful ruler and a dependent vassal group. The ruler promises benefits and protection to the vassal group, and by the vassal groups remaining loyal to the suzerain through law keeping, the covenant is maintained.[38] The background study of law and covenant in the ANE world reveals that law was not unfamiliar to the Hebrew people. In studying the content and form of ANE law, scholars have gained helpful categories for interpreting the function of the Old Testament law and the nature of God's relationship to Israel.[39]

In background studies in the New Testament, four categories of Jewish writings that were maintained from the Intertestamental period are: (1) the Jewish Apocrypha and Pseudepigrapha, (2) Philo and Josephus, (3) the Dead Sea Scrolls, and (4) rabbinic writings (Mishnah and Talmud—although these were not put into writing until much later, they still provide insights to life in Second Temple Judaism).[40] Recent scholarship has focused on the Dead Sea

---

[37] John H. Walton and Andrew E. Hill, *A Survey of the Old Testament* (Grand Rapids, MI: Zondervan, 2009), 63.

[38] Walton and Hill, *A Survey of the Old Testament*, 63.

[39] The traditional headings for ANE law are: civil law, ceremonial law, and cultic law. Christopher Wright, in *Old Testament Ethics for the People of God* (Downers Grove, IL: InterVarsity, 2004), categorizes Old Testament law into these categories: criminal law, civil law, family law, and compassionate law (cf. Walton and Hill, *Survey of the Old Testament*, 63).

[40] Brown, *Scripture as Communication*, 196.

Scrolls, which were discovered in the caves of Qumran by the Dead Sea in 1947.[41] The study of these fragments unlocks Jewish life in Intertestamental Judaism because the fragments reveal how the Qumran community, one of several Jewish sects, saw themselves as true Israel and formed their life and community through their interpretation of the Old Testament. The Dead Sea Scrolls help us understand how a Jewish sect expected the arrival of God's kingdom and waited for the restoration of Israel, near and during the time of Jesus's life and ministry.[42]

3. CRITICAL TOOLS

Critical tools, or biblical criticism, refer to the several methodologies that are formed to analyze and thoroughly interpret the biblical text. The tools in modern biblical criticism developed during the Enlightenment, when the scientific and historical analysis of literature and ancient text was applied to the study of the Bible.[43] Even though critical tools may seem like negative weapons against Scripture, and can veer toward challenging the authority of Scripture, critical tools can also be applied positively. Because God inspired the writing of Scripture in and through the lives and circumstances of human beings, analysis of Scripture as literature and as a significant ancient text is necessary for interpreting God's revelation.[44]

There are two areas of critical tools: higher and lower criticism. Lower criticism analyzes the preservation and transmission of the biblical text in the discipline called *text criticism*. A text critic applies principles and rules for comparing existing Old Testament and New Testament manuscripts and for understanding the transmission process of the biblical text. Since we do not have

---

[41] Scott, *Jewish Backgrounds of the New Testament*, 217.
[42] Scott, *Jewish Backgrounds of the New Testament*, 228.
[43] Mark Strauss, "Introducing the Bible," in *The IVP Introduction to the Bible*, ed. Philip S. Johnson (Downers Grove, IL: InterVarsity, 2006), 3.
[44] Strauss, "Introducing the Bible," 3.

any surviving original documents of the biblical authors, and the existing manuscripts of the original documents were hand-copied, the documents are susceptible to errors of copyists. The goal is to discover the causes of error in copying the original text and to reconstruct the original text of Scripture as accurately as possible.[45] Even though it is impossible to completely restore the original text of Scripture, scholars today agree, "The text of the Bible has been preserved and restored with a very high degree of reliability."[46] Most English versions of the Bible accept the Masoretic text (MT), which is the standard Hebrew text of the Old Testament.[47] With regard to the New Testament, the Nestle-Aland and United Bible Societies are considered the two standard texts. Text criticism also leads to exegetical insights of the biblical text because it requires the critic to focus on the biblical author's style, thought, and argument.[48]

Higher criticism can be divided into two main categories: historical criticism and literary criticism. Historical criticism analyzes the formation of the biblical text; this discipline consists of three movements: source, form, and redaction criticism.[49] In Gospel studies, these tools are applied to analyze the literary interrelationship between the Synoptic Gospels (Matthew, Mark, Luke). Source critics attempt to determine which Gospel was written first and was used as a source for the other synoptic writers.[50] Form critics analyze the subunits of different literary forms (i.e., parables) that make up the whole of a biblical book.[51] Because we do not live in an oral society, it is important to note that the stories of Jesus, for example, existed in oral form (tradition) first and were shaped

[45] Craig Blomberg, *Jesus and the Gospels: An Introduction and Survey* (Nashville: B&H, 2009), 83.
[46] Strauss, "Introducing the Bible," 6.
[47] Strauss, "Introducing the Bible," 6. Ancient documents such as the Samaritan Pentateuch and the Dead Sea Scrolls are helpful witnesses of the text of the Old Testament because they contain versions and fragments of the books of the Old Testament.
[48] Michael W. Holmes, "Textual Criticism," in *Interpreting the New Testament: Essays on Methods and Issues*, ed. David A. Black and David S. Dockery (Nashville: B&H, 2001), 64.
[49] Brown, *Scripture as Communication*, 281.
[50] Brown, *Scripture as Communication*, 282.
[51] Blomberg, *Jesus and the Gospels*, 93.

by the life situation of the community before authors put them into literary form. Redaction criticism analyzes how each biblical author edited his use of sources to communicate his literary and theological purpose to a particular setting.[52] By comparing each Synoptic Gospel, it is evident that each author contributes unique emphases about Jesus's life, even though they often share the same material.[53] Even though scholars can employ historical criticism and undermine the inspiration of the text, historical criticism can be used positively to understand "the ordinary human means of writing that God's Spirit superintended so as to ensure that the final product was exactly what God wanted to communicate to His people (2 Pet. 1:21)."[54]

Literary criticism builds off historical criticism and analyzes the features of the biblical text in its final form.[55] Since there are three components to a literary text (author, reader, and the text itself), each method of literary criticism has one of these components as its basis for understanding the meaning of the text.[56] Rhetorical criticism is an example of an author-centered approach, for it analyzes "how authors use literary devices to persuade or influence readers."[57] Text-centered approaches include narrative criticism, structuralism, and post-structuralism, and these claim that "meaning does not reside in the author's intention or in a reader's response" but in the structure and form of the text.[58] Reader-centered approaches include reader-response criticism (or audience criticism) and liberationist or feminist criticism. These approaches seek to read the text and arrive at the meaning from the vantage point of different audiences, such as women, the rich, the poor, and different minority groups.[59]

---

[52] Brown, *Scripture as Communication*, 282.
[53] Grant R. Osborne, "Redaction Criticism," in *Interpreting the New Testament: Essays on Methods and Issues*, ed. David A. Black and David S. Dockery (Nashville: B&H, 2001), 142.
[54] Blomberg, *Jesus and the Gospels*, 92.
[55] Strauss, "Introducing the Bible," 4.
[56] Jeffrey A. D. Weima, "Literary Criticism," in *Interpreting the New Testament: Essays on Methods and Issues*, ed. David A. Black and David S. Dockery (Nashville: B&H, 2001), 151.
[57] Strauss, "Introducing the Bible," 5.
[58] Strauss, "Introducing the Bible," 4.
[59] Strauss, "Introducing the Bible," 5.

4. RELATIONSHIP OF OLD AND NEW TESTAMENTS

The unfolding story of God's covenant relationship with Israel in the Old Testament is the primary backdrop to the world and lives of New Testament writers. Studies in the relationship of Old Testament and New Testament address the frequent times that New Testament authors echo the Old Testament story and language, which is referred to as the phenomenon of intertextuality. For example, attention to intertextuality in the "I am" passages in the Gospel of John with Old Testament imagery will aid one's interpretation of Jesus's sayings and reveal how Jesus fulfills the Old Testament teaching when he says, "I am the good shepherd," or "I am the true vine" (John 10:11; 15:1).[60]

Secondly, studies in the relationship of the Old Testament and New Testament particularly address the New Testament's direct use of Old Testament passages. The New Testament authors frequently appeal to the Old Testament "to make a theological point, to confirm a prophetic fulfillment, or to ground one ethical exhortation or another."[61] Studies in New Testament exegesis have demonstrated that some New Testament authors seem to quote Old Testament passages without a straightforward awareness of the Old Testament context,[62] and they add a new referent to the Old Testament passage. For example, Matthew interprets the birth of Jesus as a fulfillment of Isaiah 7:14, "All this took place to fulfill what the Lord had spoken by the prophet: 'Behold, the virgin shall conceive and bear a son, and they shall call his name Immanuel'" (Matt. 1:22–23). A study of Matthew's use of Isaiah 7:14 will address Matthew's interpretive method for declaring the birth of Jesus as a fulfillment of Isaiah 7:14. How is Matthew referring to Jesus when he points to the "son" in Isaiah 7:14? The context of Isaiah reveals that the son would be born at the time of Assyria's invasion of Judah (Isa. 7:17) during

---

[60] Fee, *New Testament Exegesis*, 102.
[61] Jonathan Lunde and Kenneth Berding, eds., *Three Views on the New Testament Use of the Old Testament* (Grand Rapids, MI: Zondervan, 2010), 8.
[62] Fee, *New Testament Exegesis*, 102.

Isaiah's generation and that he would be a sign of God's impending judgment on Judah. Isaiah does not seem to be prophesying about a future birth that would take place when Israel is under the power of Rome, which is the political climate in which Jesus was born. In addition to addressing the interpretive method of New Testament authors, biblical scholars in this area of research also carefully study the historical-cultural context of Old Testament passages that are quoted in the New Testament and discuss different perspectives of divine and human authorial intent. To further explain the last element, biblical scholars discuss the relationship between the intended meaning of the Old Testament and New Testament author in light of the new referent that the New Testament authors add. What is Isaiah's intended meaning for the "son" in Isaiah 7:14? Does he intend for his readers to refer to the "son" as Jesus, or does he only intend for readers to understand "son" in his historical-cultural context? What is the intended meaning of the divine author when reading a text like Isaiah 7:14 and Matthew 1:22–23?

According to Luke, Jesus is the interpretive key to the use of the Old Testament because Jesus taught the New Testament authors and the early Christians that he is the fulfillment of Moses, the Prophets, and the Psalms (Luke 24:26–27).[63] As witnesses of the resurrection, the apostles preached Jesus as the fulfillment of the Old Testament from the beginning of the church's life (e.g., Acts 1:21–22; 2:24–36; 3:12–16; 4:8–11; 5:29–31). An interpretive method for the New Testament use of the Old Testament requires attention to these elements: (1) text form, (2) hermeneutical assumptions, and (3) Jewish exegetical methods used by New Testament authors.

(1) Text Form: The New Testament authors quote from both the Masoretic Hebrew text and the Septuagint (LXX), the Greek translation of the Old Testament.

(2) Hermeneutical Assumptions: *Corporate solidarity* is an expression of the Semitic idea, "a single member of a community

---

[63] Lunde and Berding, *Three Views on the New Testament Use of the Old Testament*, 8.

can represent the whole."[64] Jesus, being Israel's representative, is the "Servant," a term first applied to Israel (Isa. 42:1; Matt. 12:18). *Correspondence in history* is the presupposition that events in history are a "type," or foreshadowing, of what God will do in the future. This assumption presupposes that God is in control of all history and that he expresses his will in and through history. For example, there is correspondence between David's suffering (Ps. 22) and Jesus's suffering on the cross (Matt. 27:39–46).[65] *Inaugurated fulfillment of Scripture* is the presupposition that the New Testament authors believed that the Old Testament expectations of the kingdom of God are fulfilled in Jesus, even though the kingdom of God is not yet fully realized. They also viewed the Old Testament to be Christological, meaning that Jesus is the goal and complete fulfillment of God's promises.[66]

(3) Jewish Exegetical Methods: *Pesher* is a Jewish method of exegesis that begins with a person or event in the New Testament, points to an Old Testament person or event, and provides a solution for understanding an Old Testament text.[67] For example, Peter preaches that the outpouring of the Spirit (Acts 2:17) points to what God was promising in Joel 2:28. *Midrash* is a method that seeks to provide explanation and exposition of a given text. It basically communicates, "That has relevance to this." For example, Jesus approved of his disciples when they ate grain on the Sabbath by explaining their action on the basis of David, who ate the bread of the Presence (Matt. 12:1–8).

5. ANCIENT AND FUTURE ISRAEL

The topic of ancient and future Israel is a historical and theological issue that interacts with "the people of God," a theme that appears

[64] Darrell L. Bock, "Use of the Old Testament in the New," in *Foundations for Biblical Interpretation: A Complete Library of Tools and Resources*, ed. David S. Dockery, Kenneth A. Mathews, and Robert B. Sloan (Nashville: B&H, 1994), 102.
[65] Klyne Snodgrass, "The Use of the Old Testament in the New," in *Interpreting the New Testament: Essays on Methods and Issues*, ed. David A. Black and David S. Dockery (Nashville: B&H, 2001), 215.
[66] Bock, "Use of the Old Testament in the New," 104.
[67] Snodgrass, "The Use of the Old Testament in the New," 218.

throughout Scripture.[68] The term "people of God" refers to Israel in the Old Testament. For example, God spoke to Moses regarding the Israelites who were enslaved in Egypt: "Say therefore to the people of Israel . . . *I will take you to be my people*, and I will be your God" (Ex. 6:6–7). Then, in the New Testament, the term "people of God" refers to the church, for Paul quotes Old Testament passages about God's covenant relationship with Israel and applies it to the church (Rom. 9:25; 2 Cor. 6:16–17). Furthermore, writing to Christians in the Diaspora, Peter says, "You are . . . a people for his own possession. . . . Once you were not a people, but now you are God's people" (1 Pet. 2:9–10). A way in which the Old Testament relates to the New Testament is by the continuity of "the people of God," which appears first in the old covenant, and then in the new covenant. God is the author of both covenants, they are both based on the Torah, and they are both established with the house of Israel (Jer. 31:31–34).[69] God's act and plan of establishing a covenant relationship with his people stretches all the way from Genesis 17:7 to Revelation 21:7.[70]

The continuity of "the people of God" between the old and new covenant is also characterized by discontinuity. In the New Testament, Jesus chooses twelve apostles, who symbolize the twelve tribes of Israel. He comes as the Messiah of Israel, but Israel rejects Jesus. Jesus seemingly turns to establish a new people of God, the church, with these twelve apostles in order to fulfill the mandate that was originally entrusted to Israel, namely, to be a light to the Gentiles (Isa. 42:6). The study of ancient and future Israel engages

---

[68] Walter Kaiser Jr., *Recovering the Unity of the Bible: One Continuous Story, Plan, and Purpose* (Grand Rapids, MI: Zondervan, 2009), 111.

[69] Kaiser, *Recovering the Unity of the Bible*, 115. Even though "the people of God" primarily referred to the people of Israel in the Old Testament, the Old Testament did not limit the term to Israel alone. In the Old Testament, God revealed through his prophets and kings that God's plan was also to include the Gentiles in a covenant relationship. Cf. similarly, David L. Baker, *Two Testaments, One Bible: The Theological Relationship between the Old and New Testaments* (Downers Grove, IL: InterVarsity, 2010), 223.

[70] Kaiser, *Recovering the Unity of the Bible*, 111: Genesis 17:7–8; Exodus 6:7; 19:5–6; Leviticus 26:11–12; Deuteronomy 4:20; 2 Samuel 7:24; 1 Chronicles 17:22; Jeremiah 31:33; Hosea 2:23; Romans 9:25; 2 Corinthians 6:16–17; 1 Peter 2:9–10; Revelation 21:3; 21:7.

these questions: (1) What is the relationship between Israel and the church? (2) Who are the people of God? (3) What happened to ancient Israel? (4) Is there a future for Israel in light of God's promise in the Old Testament and also Israel's rejection of Jesus? Though there is a wide spectrum of views regarding Israel and the church, and the future of Israel, the following are two main views.

The first view emphasizes a strong continuity between the Old and New Testament. Because Jesus and the New Testament authors apply Old Testament passages about Israel to the church, this view concludes that the church replaces Israel and is the new Israel. The remnant of Israel who believe in Jesus as Messiah form the Israel of God (Gal. 6:16) and the commonwealth of Israel (Eph. 2:12) and are a part of the church.[71] With regards to God's purpose in human history, this view does not affirm a future for Israel,[72] where posterity and the land promised to Abraham are restored to the people of ethnic Israel. God's reign is fundamentally a spiritual reign over his people, involving forgiveness of sins and life in the Holy Spirit.[73] The promises of an earthly reign, involving land and a messianic King, will be fulfilled in the new earth, and not during this age. This view that the church replaces Israel and that there is no future restoration for the nation of Israel is known as supersessionism or replacement theology.

The second view emphasizes discontinuity between the two testaments and recognizes that God's plan of salvation is twofold. Within God's unified purpose in human history, he has an earthly purpose for Israel and a heavenly purpose for the church.[74] The age of the church is a parenthetic period between the establishment of his purpose through Israel and the fulfillment of God's promises to Israel.[75] This view affirms that there is a future for the nation

---

[71] Baker, *Two Testaments, One Bible*, 225.

[72] Robert L. Saucy, *The Case for Progressive Dispensationalism: The Interface Between Dispensational and Non-Dispensational Theology* (Grand Rapids, MI: Zondervan, 1993), 23.

[73] Saucy, *The Case for Progressive Dispensationalism*, 21.

[74] Saucy, *The Case for Progressive Dispensationalism*, 25.

[75] Saucy, *The Case for Progressive Dispensationalism*, 26.

of Israel. God not only brings about spiritual redemption through Jesus Christ for Jews and Gentiles, but he will also bring about earthly redemption for the nation of Israel. Even though Israel rejected Christ and went through a period of hardening, there will be a future for Israel because God established an everlasting, covenant relationship with Israel, and as the apostle Paul writes, "The gifts and the calling of God are irrevocable" (Rom. 11:29).

The study of ancient and future Israel in relationship to the church requires careful and thorough historical-grammatical methodology in biblical interpretation. The way in which Christians understand God's plan for Israel in human history depends on how one reads Scripture with attention to the elements of continuity and discontinuity, and grasps the way in which "the people of God" is one of many biblical themes that unites the Old and New Testaments.

6. SECOND TEMPLE JUDAISM

During the four hundred years between the close of the Old Testament and the beginning of the New Testament, many political, religious, and social developments took place that shaped Jewish society.[76] The study of Jewish life in this period is called Intertestamental history, or Second Temple Judaism. This period spans from the rebuilding of the temple in Jerusalem in 515 BC to the destruction of Jerusalem in AD 70. By the beginning of this period, the northern kingdom of Israel had been destroyed by Assyria in 722 BC. As a result of covenant unfaithfulness, the temple was destroyed and the southern kingdom of Judah became exiles in Babylon in 586 BC. Seventy years later (515 BC), when the Jews were under Persian rule, Cyrus the Great permitted the Jews to return to their homeland. Though the Jews did not have the freedom to rule politically, they were permitted to rebuild the

---

[76] Carl Mosser, "Between the Testaments," *The IVP Introduction to the Bible*, ed. Philip S. Johnston (Downers Grove, IL: IVP Academic, 2006), 141.

temple. During the Second Temple period, the Jews lost national power, became a vassal state and were subject to the rule of foreign empires (Babylonian, Persian, Greek, and Roman rule). They attempted to preserve devotion to the law even though foreign beliefs and culture were constantly challenging their ethnic and religious identity. The variety of sources related to the history and culture of Second Temple Judaism provides the social, political, and religious backdrop for reading the New Testament.

The Old Testament is the most important literature for a background of the New Testament. Jesus upholds the authority of the Old Testament and does not quote from any other source (Matt. 5:18).[77] Aside from the authoritative Old Testament Scriptures, one major collection of books among Second Temple literature is the Apocrypha, which consists of a variety of writings from different literary genres, such as histories, novels, wisdom literature, and prayers, and is primarily about Jewish life and thought.[78] A source that provides valuable information on Jewish history is the *Jewish Antiquities*, a twenty-one-volume work written by Flavius Josephus, a first-century historian who wrote to a non-Jewish audience. About half of the *Antiquities* is a survey of the history of the Jewish people as they lived under Persian, Hellenistic, and Roman rule.[79] The writings of Philo of Alexandria, a Judean philosopher, are also sources about Jewish life during Second Temple Judaism. These writings all mention and provide information about how Jews were united, and divided, and about the law (Torah) and the traditions of the elders, which were central factors to Judaism.[80] For example, one of the writings in the Apocrypha, the books of the Maccabees, describes the disputes

[77] Walter A. Elwell and Robert Yarbrough, *Encountering the New Testament: A Historical and Theological Survey* (Grand Rapids, MI: Baker, 2013), 44.

[78] Elwell and Yarbrough, *Encountering the New Testament*, 44.

[79] Steve Mason, "Josephus," in *The Eerdmans Dictionary of Early Judaism*, ed. John J. Collins and Daniel C. Harlow (Grand Rapids, MI: Eerdmans, 2010), 834.

[80] Daniel Falk, "Sabbath," in *The Eerdmans Dictionary of Early Judaism*, ed. John J. Collins and Daniel C. Harlow (Grand Rapids, MI: Eerdmans, 2010), 1174.

among Jewish sects about Sabbath regulation. Because the Jews were living under the reign of foreign power, keeping their religious identity was difficult. As a result, some people wanted to abolish the Sabbath laws, and others wanted to strengthen the Sabbath laws.[81]

Another collection of writings is the Pseudepigrapha, which are Jewish writings, some of which are falsely attributed to ancient Jewish heroes. Many of these documents provide information about the theology of the Jews.[82] They allow us to understand how Jewish people viewed "God and the world, humanity, sin, judgment, kingdom of God and the future."[83]

During the Hasmonean dynasty (166–63 BC), Jewish sects such as the Pharisees, Essenes, and Sadducees arose as a result of religious and political conflicts among Jews regarding the temple. The temple was another central factor to Judaism, for it was the means by which Jews practiced worship to God and tried to establish rule and power as they hoped to become an independent nation. Jewish parties are mentioned in Josephus and Philo. Pharisees and Sadducees appear also in the New Testament and rabbinic literature, but the Essenes do not. Instead, the Essenes are "identified with or related to the group behind the Qumran library," and they are possibly the writers of the Dead Sea Scrolls.[84] Even though the origin of these parties is unknown, their development during the Hasmonean dynasty is "a result of their different levels of active participation in the makeup of the emerging new Jewish state, based on varying interpretations of the Torah and their application to the social, religious, and political agendas."[85] Even though they differed in their interpreta-

---

[81] Falk, "Sabbath," 1174.

[82] John J. Collins, "Early Judaism in Modern Scholarship," in *The Eerdmans Dictionary of Early Judaism*, ed. John J. Collins and Daniel C. Harlow (Grand Rapids, MI: Eerdmans, 2010), 7.

[83] Elwell and Yarbrough, *Encountering the New Testament*, 45.

[84] Jorg Freg, "Essenes," in *The Eerdmans Dictionary of Early Judaism*, ed. John J. Collins and Daniel C. Harlow (Grand Rapids, MI: Eerdmans, 2010), 599.

[85] Roland Deines, "Pharisees," in *The Eerdmans Dictionary of Early Judaism*, ed. John J. Collins and Daniel C. Harlow (Grand Rapids, MI: Eerdmans, 2010), 1062.

tion of the laws, they had great concern for maintaining the law because their future as a nation depended on their faithfulness to the law, and they hoped for the restoration of Israel from foreign power. The Dead Sea Scrolls reveal how the group at Qumran, possibly the Essenes, interpreted the law and lived as the righteous ones who were waiting for the coming of the Messiah and the kingdom of God. From the Babylonian exile to the rule of Herod, the Jews hoped for a king like David to arise from within Israel to restore the kingdom of Israel and to reign as the Lord's Anointed, the Messiah. Their messianic hope was rooted in the Old Testament (Gen. 49:10–11; Num. 24:17; Isa. 11:1–9), in which the Lord promised, "A star shall come out of Jacob, and a scepter shall rise out of Israel" (Num. 24:17).

The last collection of writings that is valuable for studies in Second Temple Judaism is the rabbinic literature that developed over six centuries called the Talmud, which comprises of "Pharisaic teaching gathered over the centuries."[86] Within the Talmud, there is the Mishnah, which consists of a record of the sayings of rabbis. A contemporary issue today engages with whether or not the Talmud is reliable for providing information about Jewish sages during Second Temple Judaism. Even though rabbis did not arise until after the Second Temple period, they are similar to the teachers among Jewish sects and bear strong resemblance to the Pharisees, Essenes, and Sadducees.[87]

7. THE QUEST FOR THE HISTORICAL JESUS

Because the Gospels are God-inspired accounts of the life and ministry of Jesus Christ, believers have trusted the eyewitness accounts of the Gospel writers for knowing Jesus. Even though the stories of Jesus's life are not precisely told in the same way among the Gospels, it has been widely understood that the authors considered

---

[86] Elwell and Yarbrough, *Encountering the New Testament*, 46.
[87] Richard Kalmin, "Rabbis," in *The Eerdmans Dictionary of Early Judaism*, ed. John J. Collins and Daniel C. Harlow (Grand Rapids, MI: Eerdmans, 2010), 1132.

Jesus's life "from different angles and were emphasizing different things."[88] In the late eighteenth century, the reliability of the Gospels for knowing Jesus became highly questioned due to the rationalistic spirit of the Enlightenment movement. Many biblical scholars in European universities abandoned the inspired nature of the Gospels and claimed that the truthfulness of the Gospels should be judged by rational, scientific methods.[89] The stories of Jesus became subject to different interpretive options and were viewed as legends, myths, or embellished accounts of Jesus, written many years after Jesus's earthly life by people who did not know him.[90] The search for what can be deemed as historically accurate about the life of Jesus came to be known as the quest for the historical Jesus, which can be divided into three stages.

a. Old Quest (seventeenth to mid-twentieth century): For most Enlightenment thinkers, any supernatural account in the Gospels, such as miracles, the virgin birth, and the resurrection, are either rejected as historical or need to be reinterpreted in a historical way. The supernatural accounts of Jesus's life are additions made by human authors or the community of early believers on the basis of their faith. As a result of this critique, scholars differentiated the "Christ of faith" from the "Jesus of history." Several attempts at reconstructing the life of the historical Jesus were published in the nineteenth and twentieth centuries, such as David Friedrich Strauss's *Life of Jesus Critically Examined* and Albert Schweitzer's *The Quest of the Historical Jesus*, in which he concluded that no author has discovered the Jesus of history.[91]

Rudolf Bultmann initiated a second phase in the quest of the historical Jesus. He claimed that even though there is no literal truth in the supernatural stories of Jesus, they can become true

[88] Elwell and Yarbrough, *Encountering the New Testament*, 168.
[89] Elwell and Yarbrough, *Encountering the New Testament*, 168.
[90] Michael J. Wilkins and J. P. Moreland, *Jesus Under Fire: Modern Scholarship Reinvents the Historical Jesus* (Grand Rapids, MI: Zondervan, 1995), 1–15.
[91] Elwell and Yarbrough, *Encountering the New Testament*, 170.

if modern readers incorporate their own self-understanding and de-mythologize them. However, Bultmann's methodology was rejected as "an intellectual system of faith devoid of any historical basis and in danger of losing Jesus entirely."[92]

b. New Quest (1950–1980s): Determined to maintain interest in Jesus's earthly life and his centrality in Christianity, scholars Ernst Käsemann, Ernst Fuchs, and Gunther Bornkamm began the new quest, in which they investigated Jesus's preaching in order to understand the Jesus of history.[93] In the English-speaking world, Norman Perrin critiqued the new quest and viewed that the historical knowledge of Jesus needs to be distinguished from the Christ who is preached. The methods of the new quest were still close to the existential approach of Bultmann, however, and neglected to understand the historical Jesus in light of first century Judaism.[94]

c. Third Quest (late twentieth century): The third quest went in significantly different directions. One major pursuit sought to find the historical Jesus by focusing on Jesus within his historical Jewish context. Other scholars assumed that the real words of Jesus are buried under the editorial additions made by the final authors of the Gospels, and therefore sought to find the "real" words of Jesus.[95] Some radical critical scholars formed a group called the Jesus Seminar, and by employing their methods and criteria for judging the authenticity of Jesus's words, they concluded that 82 percent of the words ascribed to Jesus in the Gospels were not actually spoken by him. This conclusion has led those in the Jesus Seminar to deny that Jesus is the Son of God, was born of a virgin, was crucified, and was resurrected. The collection of sayings that Jesus may have said, according to the scholars of the Jesus Seminar, reveal that he was most likely a religious teacher or wise sage.[96]

---

[92] Elwell and Yarbrough, *Encountering the New Teastament*, 170.
[93] Colin Brown, "Quest of the Historical Jesus," in *Dictionary of Jesus and the Gospels*, ed. J. Green, S. McKnight, and I. H. Marshall (Downers Grove, IL: InterVarsity Press, 1992), 336.
[94] Brown, "Quest of the Historical Jesus," 336.
[95] Elwell and Yarbrough, *Encountering the New Testament*, 172.
[96] Wilkins and Moreland, *Jesus Under Fire*, 1–15.

In engaging with this contemporary issue, a biblical studies student must remember that there are limits to historical research, for we cannot have absolute certainty about any event or saying in Jesus's life. However, historical research with appropriate methodologies, and with the foundational assumption that God's inspiration superintended the writers, can help us to view the Gospels with a high degree of reliability. A necessary posture for students in Gospel studies is one that embraces two types of knowing.[97] We can know Jesus subjectively. He is our Savior and Lord whom we walk with daily. We can also know Jesus historically, which entails knowing the messianic agenda of his life and ministry. By embracing these two approaches of knowing, history becomes a tool for strengthening one's faith, and faith enhances history so that it is not merely facts about the past.[98]

8. THE NEW PERSPECTIVE ON PAUL

A contemporary issue in New Testament scholarship is Paul's view of the law. Interpreters of Paul's letters have traditionally viewed justification by faith as the center of Paul's theology. In teaching about the righteousness of God, Paul writes, "For we hold that one is justified by faith apart from works of the law" (Rom. 3:28). Paul views the law as holy, righteous, and worthy of his delight (Rom. 7:12, 22), but he warns, particularly in Romans and Galatians, that law-keeping is not sufficient for salvation.[99] Martin Luther interpreted Paul's doctrine of justification by faith as a reaction to the Jews who required observation of the law as a merit for salvation. As Paul protested against the legalism in the Judaism of his day, Luther protested against the Catholic Church, which spread the same kind of teaching and practice.

Around 1975, a debate arose called the "new perspective" on

[97] Wilkins and Moreland, *Jesus Under Fire*, 231–32.
[98] For a marked contrast, see the discussion in N. T. Wright and Marcus Borg, *The Meaning of Jesus: Two Visions* (New York: HarperCollins, 1999), 26.
[99] Elwell and Yarbrough, *Encountering the New Testament*, 242.

Paul that reinterprets Paul's view of the law and the nature of justification.[100] The key scholars of the new perspective are E. P.
Sanders, James Dunn, N. T. Wright, and Krister Stendahl.[101] New
perspective scholars reject the view that first-century Judaism was
a legalistic, works-righteousness religion. Thus, Luther's view of
Paul's doctrine of justification by faith gives a negative portrayal
of Judaism.[102] As a result of studying Palestinian Judaism in the
first century, E. P. Sanders argues that Jews in Second Temple Judaism did not view law-keeping as the way to enter salvation. The
law must be understood in the framework of covenant, with the
concept of "covenantal nomism." Covenantal nomism expresses
the idea that works of the law are not a means of entering into
the covenant, but they are necessary to maintain standing in the
covenant.[103] In a slightly different direction, James D. G. Dunn un-
derstands works of the law as "badges" for staying in the covenant.
The works of the law function as proper responses to one's election
and membership in God's covenant community.[104]

Even though he agrees with Sanders's general understanding
of Judaism, Dunn argues that Paul did not have a problem with the
law, but he protested against using the law as a social barrier to reject Gentiles from entering into the covenant community of God.[105]
The old perspective views "works of the law" as good works that
are stipulated in God's law. However, Dunn proposes the view that
"works of the law," according to Paul, refer to the ethnic boundary
markers that distinguish Jewish people from the Gentiles. Thus,
the works of the law are laws that pertain to circumcision, food
laws, and Sabbath observance. By teaching that a person is not
justified by works (Gal. 2:16), Paul was teaching that a person is

---

[100] Elwell and Yarbrough, *Encountering the New Testament*, 242.

[101] Elwell and Yarbrough, *Encountering the New Testament*, 250.

[102] James D. G. Dunn, *The Theology of Paul the Apostle* (Grand Rapids, MI: Eerdmans, 1998), 338.

[103] E. P. Sanders, *Paul and Palestinian Judaism: A Comparison of Patterns of Religion* (Philadelphia, PA: Fortress, 1977), 75.

[104] James D. G. Dunn, *Jesus, Paul, and the Law: Studies in Mark and Galatians* (Louisville, KY: Westminster / John Knox, 1900), 191–96.

[105] Dunn, *Jesus, Paul, and the Law*, 191–96.

not counted righteous on the basis of these boundary markers, or "a nationalistic misuse of the Law."[106]

The value of new perspective study is that it corrects the view that first-century Judaism was fundamentally legalistic.[107] It has caused New Testament scholarship to research the history of Second Temple Judaism more thoroughly so that our view of Judaism today does not misrepresent or generalize Judaism. Also, as many distinguished scholars continue extensive research on Paul's view of the law and justification by faith, the hope is that our understanding of the gospel, our interpretation of Romans and Galatians, the meaning of the righteousness of God, and the role of works in salvation and the Christian life will deepen.[108] Still it is important to recognize that evangelical scholarship, while seeking to learn from and engage the work of Sanders, Dunn, Wright, and others, has largely continued to affirm the essence of the Reformation doctrine of justification by faith. Helpful guidance in this regard may be found in *Justification and the New Perspectives on Paul* by Guy Prentiss Waters (P&R, 2004).

9. BIBLICAL THEOLOGY AND THEOLOGICAL READING OF THE BIBLE

Biblical theology is a discipline that attempts to describe the unifying message of the Bible with careful attention to the diversity in the biblical material. In order to grasp the theological heart of the Bible, biblical theologians interact with themes that can be traced throughout the whole Bible and discuss how those themes relate to one another.[109] It is common among biblical scholars to study the theology of a biblical author, a biblical book, the Old Testament or the New Testament. Biblical theology seeks to understand the overarching theology of the whole Bible as it develops from Genesis to Revelation.

---

[106] Dunn, *Jesus, Paul, and the Law*, 200.

[107] Richard Longenecker, *Galatians* (Nashville: Thomas Nelson, 1990), 86.

[108] See observations of Frank Thielmann, "Law," in *Dictionary of Paul and His Letters*, ed. Gerald F. Hawthorne and Ralph P. Martin (Downers Grove, IL: InterVarsity Press, 1993), 529–32.

[109] Scott J. Hafemann and Paul R. House, eds., *Central Themes in Biblical Theology: Mapping Unity in Diversity* (Grand Rapids, MI: Baker Academic, 2007), 16.

The motivation behind biblical theology is the foundational assumption, "The Bible is a unity because it is the word of God, who is a unified and coherent being."[110] However, the unity of the Bible is not characterized by uniformity. The unity of the Bible is characterized by diversity. There are different genres and theological purposes among biblical authors. Diversity in Scripture does not negate its unity; rather, the unity of the Bible is supported by diverse words and forms.[111] Biblical theology is a descriptive discipline in that it seeks to study God's self-revelation as it was given in its historical context, according to the final form of the text, and in order from the Old Testament to the New Testament before arriving at a theology for contemporary thought and church doctrine.[112] The following are a few widely recognized biblical themes that span throughout the Bible and contribute to the unity of the Bible.[113]

In the twentieth century, salvation history became recognized as a biblical theme and a popular approach to biblical theology. Its basis is that the two testaments are bound together by the revelation of God's saving acts in history and the coming of Jesus as the climax of salvation history.[114] A key concept of salvation history is *typology*. Typology centers on the idea of correspondence between people, events, and institutions throughout the historical activity of God.[115] For example, the exodus is a historical event that has theological correspondence to the cross and the resurrection of Jesus. The exodus is a "type" of salvation, which is ultimately accomplished by Jesus Christ, who delivers us from slavery to sin. By identifying salvation history as the overall framework that shapes the message of the Bible, biblical theologians attempt

[110] Hafemann and House, *Central Themes in Biblical Theology*, 16.
[111] Baker, *Two Testaments, One Bible*, 233.
[112] Mark W. Elliot, *The Heart of Biblical Theology: Providence Experienced* (Burlington, VT: Ashgate, 2012), 7.
[113] Hafemann and House, *Central Themes in Biblical Theology*, 15.
[114] Baker, *Two Testaments, One Bible*, 272.
[115] Baker, *Two Testaments, One Bible*, 273.

to understand how each biblical author interpreted key events in history to fit in the salvation history theme of the Bible.[116]

Another theme in biblical theology is promise and fulfillment. The Old Testament reveals the promises of God through Abraham, David, and the prophets, and they are fulfilled in Jesus Christ in the New Testament. Biblical theology involves interpreting all of Scripture "in Christ." Even though there are differences in content between the two testaments, "the Old and New Testament are equally Christian Scripture."[117] The whole Bible revolves around the person of Jesus Christ, as Paul wrote, "For all the promises of God find their Yes in him" (2 Cor. 1:20). The New Testament provides us with a Christological interpretation of the Old Testament and reveals how the Old Testament witnesses to Christ as the Messiah.[118]

Lastly, the concept of covenant relationship is another theme in the Bible, or a subject matter of biblical theology. This approach of biblical theology involves tracing the storyline of God's covenant relationship with his people from the Old to the New Testament. Though there is more than one covenant in the Bible, the concept of covenant relationship is the "historical arena within which God reveals himself."[119] By studying the Abrahamic, Mosaic, Davidic, and new covenants, it becomes apparent that the covenant relationship is an interpretive lens that ties together the historical unity of the Bible despite its diversity.[120]

The overall goal of biblical theology is to understand the message of the Bible. The history of biblical interpretation teaches that an important element by which one should do biblical theology is the Trinitarian rule of faith. The rule of faith helps us maintain our inter-

---

[116] Roy E. Ciampa, "The History of Redemption," in *Central Themes in Biblical Theology: Mapping Unity in Diversity*, ed. Scott J. Hafemann and Paul House (Grand Rapids, MI: Baker Academic, 2007), 255.

[117] Baker, *Two Testaments, One Bible*, 271.

[118] Baker, *Two Testaments, One Bible*, 271.

[119] Scott Hafemann, "The Covenant Relationship," in *Central Themes in Biblical Theology: Mapping Unity in Diversity*, ed. Scott J. Hafemann and Paul House (Grand Rapids, MI: Baker Academic, 2007), 22.

[120] Hafemann, "The Covenant Relationship," 22.

pretation of the Bible and interaction with biblical themes around the center, which is life with Jesus Christ, by the power of the Holy Spirit and in communion with the Father.[121] When doing biblical theology, the rule of faith helps us to see that the Old Testament should be read closely together with the New Testament, for "the God of creation and covenant is also the God revealed to us in Jesus Christ."[122]

INTERPRETIVE METHOD IN BIBLICAL STUDIES

We now turn to discuss the methods that guide our interpretation of the Bible. We first clarify two foundational assumptions that will in turn guide our methods, and then we will provide an overview of the methods employed in biblical studies

A DIVINE-HUMAN BOOK

In the first place, even as our Lord Jesus Christ—the living Word of God (cf. John 1:1, 14; Rev. 19:13)—is one person in two natures, divine and human, so the Bible—the written Word of God (cf. Ex. 32:16; 2 Tim. 3:16)—is one book in two natures, divine and human: it is a divine-human book. It is divine because it was God-breathed, and it is human because God used human authors to write down his words. The Spirit of God guided and superintended the writers of Scripture so that the very words, and all of the words, contain without error the truth that God intended to communicate to humans.[123] Therefore, as we read the Bible, we are hearing God speak to us through humans, and our methods for reading it and gaining insight to its meaning will need to emphasize both aspects. Therefore, on the one hand this is a truly spiritual endeavor as we listen to God speak through the authors. And on the other hand this is an equally human endeavor as we listen through human language and interact with the written text of the

---

[121] Todd Billings, "How to Read the Bible," *Christianity Today*, October 2011: 24–30, accessed October 28, 2013, http://www.christianitytoday.com/ct/2011/october/how-to-read-bible.html.

[122] Hafemann, "The Covenant Relationship," 23.

[123] For discussion, see Wayne Grudem, *Systematic Theology: An Introduction to Biblical Doctrine* (Grand Rapids, MI: Zondervan, 1994), 47–53.

Bible much like we interact with other written texts. As we enter into the world of biblical studies, it is awe-inspiring to know that we are hearing God speak to us through humans who have been impacted by God himself, and we can be impacted directly as well.

THREE HORIZONS OF THE BIBLE

In the second place, this divine-human Bible is especially appreciated through studying three interdependent "horizons" of the text—what may be seen from a particular vantage point.[124]

These three "horizons" are:

1. The horizon of the unified record of God's activities in history.
2. The horizon of the biblical authors' diverse perspectives of God's activities in history.
3. The horizon of contemporary significance.

(1) *A unified record of God's activities in history.* One horizon views the Bible as a unified record of God's activities in *history*. Here we ask the question, "What did God do in history?" This emphasizes the Bible as a window that gives insight to God's activities in history. Here we view God's activities from the creation of this world and the men and women who would be the guardians of his creation (Gen. 1:1–28), to the consummation of this age with the creation of a new heavens and new earth (Rev. 20:11–21:1). The chief focal point for God's activity in history is Jesus the Messiah, the very God who entered history and took on human nature. On this horizon we see the activities of Jesus in his death, burial, and

---

[124] Anthony Thiselton, *New Horizons in Hermeneutics: The Theory and Practice of Transforming Biblical Reading* (Grand Rapids, MI: Zondervan, 1992), 46. The notion of "horizons" has been explored in technical senses (e.g., by Thiselton), and this has been followed by practical application in theological interpretation (e.g., Joel B. Green, *1 Peter*, The Two Horizons New Testament Commentary [Grand Rapids, MI: Eerdmans, 2007]) and in expository preaching (e.g., Sidney Greidanus, *The Modern Preacher and the Ancient Text: Interpreting and Preaching Biblical Literature* [Grand Rapids, MI: Eerdmans, 1988], 300–6). Green focuses on the horizons of theological exegesis and theological reflection. Greidanus focuses on the horizon of the historical activities in the Bible and the horizon of the author and audience, similar to the method here. Both approaches emphasize two horizons, but also include the reader's own horizon, to which I refer as the third horizon (cf. Thiselton, *New Horizons*, 604–19).

resurrection as he fulfills the promises to Israel and to the world by accomplishing salvation for his people. It is also on this horizon that we see God's future activities as he consummates his plan of salvation in the return of Jesus to gather his people into his new heavens and new earth, and brings judgment to those who have rejected him.

This historical record was the basis of the biblical authors' faith and the faith of those to whom they wrote. They wished to impart to their readers the truth of what God had done in history. For example, Luke, the author of the third Gospel, tells his reader, Theophilus, that he had carefully researched the records at hand of Jesus and the events of his life and ministry, and then wrote a careful account, "so that you may know the exact truth about the things you have been taught" (Luke 1:4 NASB).

The Bible is our primary textbook for this horizon, but in the discipline of biblical studies, this is also where we employ other evidence of history such as archaeology, secular writings, religious traditions, sociological and anthropological studies, and general revelation. These other sources put God's activities into their historical context. We will see in the next horizon that there is diversity in the various biblical authors' perspectives, but here we emphasize that this first horizon gives a unified record of God's activities in history. It is on this horizon that we place ourselves in the sweep of history to see and hear God as he brought salvation for his people, established his covenants, reconciled men and women to himself, and fulfilled his promises to us as he established his kingdom on earth.

(2) *The horizon of the biblical authors' diverse perspectives of God's activities in history*. The second horizon is the authors' diverse perspectives for diverse audiences of the record of God's activities in history. Here we ask the question, "How did the biblical authors record the meaning of God's activities in history?" This emphasizes that each author provides different perspectives as biblical windows into history that help us explore the *meaning* of God's activities. The authors of the various books of the Bible

were witnesses or recorders or prophets of the heart of the message that God has acted in history, but not only did they *record* God's activities, they clarified their *meaning* as well. For example, the authors of 1–2 Kings and 1–2 Chronicles record events that transpired over much of the same time period, but they had unique perspectives that underscore their unique purposes in writing for their individual audiences.

This is similar to the four Gospels in the New Testament. A recovery of the bare facts of history was not enough for the evangelists. They wished to so present the facts that their readers would understand the meaning of Jesus's life and ministry, that he was indeed the Christ, who is their Savior. The authors, led by the Holy Spirit, presented materials that focused on their true purpose of declaring Jesus to be the Messiah Savior. As such, they are not strictly biographies, annals, life stories, diaries, or memoirs. Rather, in the Gospels of the New Testament we have a distinct literary form, *interpreted history*, which is truly the "good news" of God to his people.[125] The apostle John tells his audience that out of the vast historical materials about Jesus's life and ministry that were available, he wrote his Gospel with a theological purpose: "These are written so that you may believe that Jesus is the Christ, the Son of God, and that by believing you may have life in his name" (John 20:31). And he likewise tells the readers of his first letter that he wrote with a similar theological purpose: "I write these things to you who believe in the name of the Son of God, that you may know that you have eternal life" (1 John 5:13). The second horizon gives us the authors' unique perspectives of the meaning of God's activities in history.

(3) *The horizon of contemporary significance.* The third horizon is the present-day reader's application and interaction with the first two horizons. Here we ask the question, "What is the contemporary significance for readers today?" This horizon explores

---

[125] For an overview of this discussion, see Larry W. Hurtado, "Gospel (Genre)," *Dictionary of Jesus and the Gospels*, ed. Joel B. Green, Scot McKnight, and I. Howard Marshall (Downers Grove, IL: InterVarsity, 1992), 276–82.

the contemporary *significance* of God's activities in history and the various authors' perspectives of his activities, and how we can apply this material to our own lives. In a sense, on this horizon we view the Bible as an open window through which we can place one foot in the biblical world while keeping the other foot firmly planted in our contemporary world, and walk with the biblical characters and apply principles and truths and warnings from their lives to our own.

We are really not that different as humans from those of the first two horizons, but there are contemporary issues and circumstances that we must address that make the reading of the Bible immediately relevant. For example, while David was the king of Israel and one of the most important historical figures of the Old Testament, many of his personal experiences in his relationship with God and other humans can speak directly into our own lives. When he was confronted by Nathan the prophet regarding his sinful adultery with Bathsheba, he wrote a psalm of repentance that is an example of repentance for all of us as he says, "For you will not delight in sacrifice, or I would give it; you will not be pleased with a burnt offering. The sacrifices of God are a broken spirit; a broken and contrite heart, O God, you will not despise" (Ps. 51:16–17). God desires from each of us not simply more religious activity, but a pure heart.

Matthew begins his Gospel by referring to Jesus as Immanuel, "God with us" (1:23), and concludes his Gospel with Jesus's declaration, "I am with you always, to the end of the age" (28:20). There is no more radical claim than understanding that Jesus is God incarnate, who came to be with his people Israel, and now in his risen and ascended position with the Father, remains with all who have followed him to gain eternal life. That was the essence of discipleship to Jesus in the first century, and remains the privilege of Christians today as we walk with Jesus in the world of the twenty-first century.

AN OVERVIEW OF THE METHODS
OF BIBLICAL STUDIES

Because the Bible is a divine-human book, we use methods in biblical studies that are similar to, yet quite unique from, those used when reading and interpreting other kinds of literature. These methods blend various elements, such as an intense academic scrutiny of the Bible and related subjects, an expository attempt to understand the particulars of biblical literature, a personal attempt by the student to come to resolutions of problem passages and introductory matters, and a spiritual quest to understand the mind of God in his purposes for having the Bible written. With these varied elements, it is supremely important for the student to apply himself or herself conscientiously to this study. It will require all of one's mental, physical, and spiritual capacities to maximize the value of this study. Never forget that the Spirit of God is at work in the mind and heart of each believer studying the Bible, that he will reward us according to our diligence of study, and that he will enlighten our minds and hearts as we prayerfully yield ourselves to his guidance.

Interpretive methods vary according to the experience and intentions of the interpreter, but several important features are core to the process.[126]

1. Texts and Scripture. As we noted above, since the Bible is a divine-human book, it is similar to, yet quite different from, other types of written texts. The science and art of "hermeneutics" (from the Greek word *hermeneuo*, "I interpret or translate") attempts to establish principles of interpretation of written texts, including the Bible. Many of the same principles apply to interpreting both secular and Christian literature, but there is an additional element when interpreting the Bible, because we understand that God is the author, but human authors were guided and superintended by God

---

[126] For a complete discussion of exegetical methodology, see Craig L. Blomberg with Jennifer Foutz Markley, *A Handbook of New Testament Exegesis* (Grand Rapids, MI: Baker Academic, 2010).

in the writing of the Bible. The Bible is not just any text, but to the Christian it is Holy Scripture. The apostle Paul gave a stirring guideline to his companion Timothy that has relevance for us as we attempt to interpret the Bible: "Do your best to present yourself to God as one approved, a worker who has no need to be ashamed, rightly handling the word of truth" (2 Tim. 2:15). We handle truth from God in the Bible.

Likewise, the science and art of "exegesis" (from the Greek words *ex*, "from, out of" and *ago*, "I lead, bring along") attempts to develop a workable process to bring out the divinely intended meaning of the Bible. These two processes overlap at many points.

2. Textual criticism. Since we do not have the original manuscripts (or "autographs"), we undertake the science of "textual criticism" in order to establish as closely as possible an accurate reconstruction of what was originally written. This gives the interpreter confidence in the accuracy and authenticity of our current texts.

3. Original languages and translation. Since those original manuscripts were written in either Hebrew, Aramaic, or Greek, we next undertake a translation of those texts if we have proficiency in the original languages, or turn to modern translations that help to clarify the authors' original intention in writing. In your studies we encourage you to gain at least basic proficiency in the original languages, because it adds a depth in your study of the Bible. But if that is not possible, adopt a good translation that will further your studies.

Today we can find a multitude of different modern translations in English (and many other modern languages) that reflect different translation objectives, ranging from literal word-to-word renderings ("formal equivalency") to thought-to-thought renderings ("dynamic equivalency"), each having their place for our different modern purposes in understanding and communicating the Bible. The translation that we use primarily in this book is the English

Standard Version, which is a most trustworthy translation that students find helpful in the study of the Bible.[127]

4. Historical-cultural contexts. Investigating historical-cultural contexts applies to both the horizon of God's actions in history as well as the horizon of the authors of the biblical books. For example, what were the circumstances in history and culture (e.g., religious, political, and military authorities; economic conditions) when Moses became the leader of the people of Israel when he led them out of Egypt? What were the religious and cultural conditions when Jesus walked and ministered in first-century Palestine? And what were the circumstances (e.g., date, location, purposes, setting) of Mark or Paul as they communicated their written messages about Jesus to their particular audiences in the extended Mediterranean world? Understanding the historical-cultural contexts of the Bible allows us to enter more fully into the experiences of the biblical figures so that we can, in a sense, walk with them throughout the events of their lives.[128]

5. Literary contexts. The literary context of any passage we are studying in the Bible includes whether it is Old or New Testament, and the various literary forms or genres such as the Law, the Prophets, the writings of the Old Testament, or the Gospels, Acts, Epistles, or Revelation of the New Testament. The literary context also includes the place of a passage within the book itself, the identification of various figures of speech, and the use of rhetoric or exhortation. All of this is important for understanding the authors' intended meaning.

6. Lexical, grammatical, and syntactical contexts. How words are used and the relationships between words are important elements in understanding each author's meaning. Words

---

[127] Andreas J. Köstenberger and David A. Croteau, eds., *Which Bible Translation Should I Use?: A Comparison of 4 Major Recent Versions* (Nashville: B&H, 2012).

[128] Craig A. Evans, *Jesus and His World: The Archaeological Evidence* (Louisville, KY: Westminster John Knox, 2012); John J. Collins and Daniel C. Harlow, eds., *The Eerdmans Dictionary of Early Judaism* (Grand Rapids, MI: Eerdmans, 2010). Many entries and introductory articles are of extreme value. See "Rabbi," etc.

change meaning over time, so it is important to understand the basic lexical sense of a word, but also how an author uses a word in a particular grammatical form in a sentence and how the author uses sentences in syntactical relationship in larger literary contexts.

7. *Interpretive problems*. Problems arise when any of the above interpretive elements can be understood in different ways. We need to see not only the evidence for each particular view, but especially employ an objective procedure for resolving those problems.

8. *Outlining*. A large part of understanding a particular passage of the Bible involves making an outline of the passage, following either the original language or a trusted translation. This helps to plot the author's narrative development or logical reasoning. Allow the Spirit to guide you as he speaks to you about the intent of the author in writing and how it is developed narratively or logically.

9. *Biblical and systematic theology*. Biblical theology arises from attempting to understand an author's purpose in writing a particular biblical passage, how that purpose relates to the whole of the biblical book within which it is found, how that relates to other themes that the author surfaces. Biblical theology is therefore derived by studying the thought and themes of an individual author or body of biblical literature, or by tracing a theme through all or a portion of the Bible. Sound biblical theology will naturally lead to sound systematic theology. The interpreter should be attentive to the basic categories of systematic theology so that one's biblical theology can inform systematic theology and therefore contribute to the overall teaching of the Bible.

10. *Application and communication*. Understanding the contemporary significance of a passage of Scripture should lead to its application in the life of the twenty-first-century reader. The more directly a biblical passage addresses situations or issues that parallel twenty-first-century situations and issues, the more likely the

application will be appropriate. But the contemporary significance of Scripture is not a private privilege; it is meant to be shared with the community of believers and also with those outside of the community who need to hear this good news.

This brief overview of the methods employed in biblical studies should help the reader to follow tested procedures and be clearer and closer to the message that God and the human authors intended to communicate to us.

3

THEOLOGICAL STUDIES

WHY STUDY THEOLOGY? THEOLOGY AS RELATIONAL-TRANSFORMATIONAL TRUTH

Just the word "doctrine" scares people.[1] They often assume it is detached from the affections and used to oppress people and rob life of joy. Apart from doctrine there would be no reason for courses, majors, colleges, or universities at all. Doctrine just means "teaching," and every discipline in a university has a set of doctrines that it teaches. Are biblical studies dry, boring, cold, clinical, and impractical? Does the academic study of the Bible lead to spiritual deadness and loss of faith? While these perceptions may be the experience of some, they need not be the norm. Understanding God's revelation should lead to understanding the joy of knowing the God who made the world and declared it very good. Theological studies are all about holistic discipleship, and they equip us to obey the Great Commandment (Matt. 22:37–40) and fulfill the Great Commission (Matt. 28:19–20).

We need not fear that increased knowledge of God is going to lead to coldness of heart or loss of faith. Having knowledge that is disconnected from our affections and daily life certainly happens, but the problem is not with the *knowledge* but with the *disconnect*. It can be very mysterious trying to figure out why our knowledge does not always translate into more faith,

---
[1] Portions of this chapter have been adapted from Erik Thoennes, *Life's Biggest Questions: What the Bible Says about the Things That Matter Most* (Wheaton, IL: Crossway, 2011), 29–36, 41–47; and Thoennes, "Biblical Doctrine: An Overview," in The ESV Study Bible®, ESV Bible® (Wheaton, IL: Crossway, 2008), 2505–7.

intimacy with God, and godliness in our lives,[2] but intimacy with God demands knowledge of him. Any thinking that draws a false dichotomy between rational propositions about God and growing in one's relationship with God fails to see the necessary connection between love and knowledge. The capacity to love a person is always increased by greater knowledge of that person. Love and knowledge go hand in hand. Good lovers are students of the beloved.

Imagine that a young man asks a young lady on a date, and over dinner she begins to open up to him and share about herself. She tells him about her background, her dreams, hopes, fears, and what makes her tick. And about ten minutes into her self-revelation, the young man says, "I want our relationship to be natural, organic, and flow from our hearts, and quite frankly, all this information about you is making it really hard to do that. It's complicating things, and I fear that all these facts about you are bogging down the natural authenticity of our relationship." I highly doubt she would even consider a second date. We can all recognize the absurdity of this young man wanting to have a meaningful relationship without earnestly seeking to *know* his date. Similarly, relationship with God depends on correct knowledge of him. Relational knowledge of God is the goal of theology. Knowledge without devotion is cold, dead orthodoxy. Devotion without knowledge is irrational instability. However, true knowledge of God includes understanding everything from his perspective. The study of theology is learning to think God's thoughts after him so that our minds and hearts and actions are conformed to his image. When we study the Bible, we seek to learn what God loves and hates, what makes him angry, and what delights his heart. Once

---

[2] A very helpful study for pondering this mystery can be found in an essay by John Coe, "The Hidden Heart: Why We Still Sin When We Know So Much," August 2, 2010, http://open.biola.edu/resources/why-we-sin-when-we-know-so-much-paper?collection=spiritual-formation-lecture-series.

we know what God is like, then we can begin to become more like him in our heads, hearts, and hands. Knowing how God thinks is the first step to godliness.

All our greatest problems can be traced back to faulty understanding of God and his ways. Divorce, pornography, war, racism, gossip, lying, pride, and everything that makes creation groan starts with getting God and his ways wrong. A. W. Tozer rightly said that the "most important thing about a man is what comes into his mind when he thinks about God."[3] This means that the study of theology deserves our greatest attention. This does not mean that the other academic disciplines are not important, just that they derive their importance from the knowledge of God. This is why the study of theology has been called "The Queen of the Sciences." I (Erik) was a philosophy major at a large state university. I never had a Christian professor in my entire time in college, but as a Christian, all my studies fueled my worship of God. Biology 110—Introduction to Human Biology—drove me to my knees in amazement at the power and wisdom of the Creator who made the cell, heart, and brain. The study of art, history, psychology, philosophy, and literature increased my awe of God and trust in him. God made everything, so everything he made is worth knowing about. Believing that a perfectly good, wise, powerful God made the world and declared it "very good" gives us a wonderfully positive view of the world, and the best reason we can find to study the liberal arts. Theological studies should not be done in isolation from the other disciplines. Our knowledge of God should inform all our other knowledge, and all our other knowledge should inform our knowledge of God. We can never fully understand anything well unless we think about it in light of the character of God and who we are as his image bearers. As Calvin wrote in the very first sentence of his famous *Institutes*, "Nearly all the wisdom

---

[3] A. W. Tozer, *Knowledge of the Holy* (New York: Harper and Row, 1961), 9.

we possess, that is to say, true and sound wisdom, consists of two parts: the knowledge of God and of ourselves."[4]

What we learn about God is intended to invade every aspect of our lives. False ideas about God ruin our lives, and this begins with the ruin of our spiritual lives and our relationship with God. Once wrong thinking about God fractures our relationship with him, everything else becomes distorted. As the great English pastor and theologian Stephen Charnock said:

> According to the weakness of our knowledge is the slightness of all our acts toward God. When we do not understand his justice, we shall presume upon him. When we are ignorant of his glorious majesty, we shall be rude with him. Unless we understand his holiness, we shall leap from sin to duty; if we are ignorant of his excellency, we shall lack humility before him. If we have not a sense of his omniscience, we shall be careless in his presence, full of roving thoughts, guilty of vain babbling as if he lacked information.[5]

Although all difficulties have their origin in thinking wrongly about God, the greatest human problem is dethroning God. Idolatry consists in "the entertainment of thoughts about God that are unworthy of Him."[6] When we make unworthy thoughts about God part of our thinking, we then fail to fulfill the primary purpose for which we were created—to glorify God. Glorifying God begins with thinking about him as he really is, because "it impossible to honor God as we ought, unless we know him as he is."[7]

A pragmatic, human-centered, therapeutic approach to life pushes the value of doctrine to the edges of importance. Al-

---

[4] John Calvin, *Institutes of the Christian Religion* (Louisville: Westminister John Knox Press, 1960, revised 2006), 1:35.

[5] Stephen Charnock, *The Complete Works of Stephen Charnock* (Edinburgh: Banner of Truth, 1853), 4:27.

[6] Tozer, *Knowledge of the Holy*, 11.

[7] Stephen Charnock, *Discourses on the Existence and Attributes of God* (New York: Carter & Brothers, 1853), 208–9.

though many other questions dominate our thinking, the most important questions are those that God himself emphasizes in the Bible. These are primarily about who God is, who we are, why he created us, and what it means to be in right relationship with our Creator. The classic categories of systematic theology (God, revelation, humanity, sin, Christ, Holy Spirit, salvation, sanctification, church, and last things) are classic because they are major themes the Bible primarily addresses. There are many other important issues the Bible talks about, but these are foundational.

By far, the "issue" the Bible seeks to explain most is God himself. Every other major question is ultimately answered by thinking rightly about God himself. So, answering the question "What is God like?" needs to be our greatest concern. This is why Emil Brunner said that there "is only one question which is really serious, and that is the question concerning the being and nature of God. From this all other questions derive their significance."[8] Only when we grow in our knowledge of God can we then understand ourselves, sin, Christ, and how God restores our relationship with him. The character of God, seen primarily in the person and work of Christ, is the heart of everything. Our lives are to be lived to the glory of God, and this glory is seen definitively in Christ (2 Cor. 4:6). Knowing Christ is *the* central truth, and this needs to be our great aim and vision (Phil. 3:10) in all our studies.

We cannot know Christ rightly unless we know him as Savior. The study of theology as God intends is a profoundly personal and relational endeavor. Without acknowledging our need for forgiveness and reconciliation with God, we can never truly know him. Of all the things Christians believe, the easiest one to prove is that we have a major sin problem in the world.

---

[8] Emil Brunner, cited in Donald G. Bloesch, *God the Almighty*, Christian Foundations (Downers Grove, IL: IVP Academic, 1995), 1.

But in spite of the overwhelming evidence for this in our broken world, our sinfulness is probably the hardest thing for us to accept. The God we find in the Bible is revealing himself as the God who is redeeming sinners and restoring his broken creation. The more we understand how bad things are, the more we can rejoice in how good God is as he makes all things new. Theology is an intellectual pursuit, but it is ultimately about restored relationship with God through the finished work of Christ. The Christian theologian should not be able to study God without passionately pursuing knowledge of the Creator and Redeemer.

DEVELOPING BIBLICAL DISCERNMENT

Many think that just being a "good" person and "loving" God, without an emphasis on doctrine, is preferable. But being a good person can mean radically different things depending on what someone thinks "good" is, or what constitutes a "person." Loving God will look very different depending on one's conception of "God" or "love." The fundamental connections between belief and behavior, and between love and knowledge, demand a rigorous pursuit of truth for those wanting to love God and to be godly. Hebrews 5:11–6:3 teaches that deepening theological understanding equips one to be able to differentiate good from evil, and it exhorts believers to mature in their knowledge of God and his ways:

> For though by this time you ought to be teachers, you need someone to teach you again the basic principles of the oracles of God. You need milk, not solid food, for everyone who lives on milk is unskilled in the word of righteousness, since he is a child. But solid food is for the mature, for those who have their powers of discernment trained by constant practice to distinguish good from evil. Therefore let us leave the elementary doctrine of Christ and go on to maturity (Heb. 5:12–6:1).

HOW TO STUDY THEOLOGY

The word *theology* comes from two Greek words, *theos* ("God") and *logos* ("word"). The study of theology strives to know God as he has revealed himself and then draw necessary implications from that knowledge in an accurate, coherent, relevant way. Evangelical theology is based in the belief that God exists, is personal, can be known, and has revealed himself. These presuppositions motivate evangelical theologians to devote themselves to a fervent pursuit of knowing and loving God according to his Word. Unfortunately, the word *theologian* is used almost exclusively for vocational theologians rather than for anyone earnestly devoted to knowing God. On one level, everyone who thinks about God is a theologian. But a believer whose life is consumed with knowing her Lord is most certainly a theologian, and theologians are committed to truth. Loving God means loving truth. God is a God of truth; he *is* truth. In Scripture, all three persons of the Trinity are vitally related to truth.

ALL THREE PERSONS OF THE TRINITY VITALLY RELATED TO TRUTH

God the Father: "He who blesses himself in the land shall bless himself by *the God of truth*, and he who takes an oath in the land shall swear by *the God of truth*; because the former troubles are forgotten and are hidden from my eyes" (Isa. 65:16).

God the Son: "Jesus said to him, 'I am the way, *and the truth, and the life*. No one comes to the Father except through me" (John 14:6).

God the Holy Spirit: "When the Helper comes, whom I will send to you from the Father, *the Spirit of Truth*, who proceeds from the Father, he will bear witness about me" (John 15:26).

"When *the Spirit of Truth* comes, he will guide you into all the truth" (John 16:13).

In light of this relationship between God and truth, it should be no surprise that the Great Commandment includes loving God with one's mind: "And you shall love the Lord your God with all your heart and with all your soul and with all your mind and with all your strength" (Mark 12:30). Loving God fully and obeying the Great Commandment require actively engaging one's mind in the pursuit of truth. The second half of the Great Commandment—love your neighbor as yourself (Mark 12:31)—also requires a great commitment to truth. Love, kindness, and compassion must include profound concern that people understand the truth since their eternal destinies depend on it. God meets our greatest need of relationship with him through an understanding of truth: "Of his own will [God] brought us forth by the word of truth, that we should be a kind of firstfruits of his creatures" (James 1:18; cf. 1 Pet. 1:23). Sanctification also happens by means of the truth: "Sanctify them in the truth; your word is truth" (John 17:17; cf. Rom. 12:2). The true test of authentic discipleship is knowing and obeying truth: "If you abide in my word, you are truly my disciples, and you will know the truth, and the truth will set you free" (John 8:31–32). Therefore, loving others involves having a deep desire that they understand truth. This is the reason the Great Commission has a vital teaching element. Making disciples of Christ involves teaching them to observe all he has commanded (Matt. 28:20). Jesus wants people to understand and obey truth and thereby find life in him. Failure to care whether or not loved ones understand the truth is failure to care about their eternal destinies as well as the true abundance of their lives this side of eternity. People are judged and go to hell because they fail to love and obey God's truth (2 Thess. 2:11–13; cf. Rom. 1:18, 21, 25; James 1:18; 1 Pet. 1:23).

THEOLOGICAL METHOD

Systematic theology seeks to summarize biblical teaching on particular topics in order to draw definitive conclusions that intersect with life. God has revealed himself to his people in human history, which is why he can be known personally. He has not only revealed himself in facts and statements, but what is objectively true of him has also been revealed in the subjective experience of historical events. The experiences God's people had with him in the biblical accounts become the basis for all believers experiencing him now.

God's revelation in history is rich, personal, and wedded to real life. It can also be more difficult to understand than mere facts and propositions because the historical context of the revelation is often foreign to modern people. Because revelation of God is personal and historical, the biblical understanding of God is progressive and cumulative. The theologian, then, must consider the historical context and progressive nature of revelation at every stage. The theological process must include careful exegesis of passages that are relevant to the question being answered. Furthermore, exegesis should be done with great sensitivity to the historical context of the passages being studied. This theological method has produced several focused areas of study.

THE THEOLOGICAL PROCESS

The theological process can be categorized under several aspects and disciplines, as shown on the chart following.[9] In particular, systematic theology builds on the conclusions of exegesis and biblical theology. It attempts to summarize the teaching of Scripture in a brief, understandable, and carefully formulated statement. It involves appropriately *collecting, synthesizing,* and *understanding* all the relevant passages in the Bible on various topics, and then *summarizing* their teachings clearly so that God's people know what to believe and how to live in relation to theological questions.

---

[9]Chart taken from Thoennes, *Life's Biggest Questions,* 34; and "Biblical Doctrine: An Overview," 2506.

The Theological Process

Exegesis	The process of seeking to determine the correct meaning out of a particular passage of Scripture.
Biblical Theology	The study of scriptural revelation based on the historical framework presented in the Bible.
Systematic Theology	A study that answers the question, "What does the whole Bible teach us today about a given topic?"
Historical Theology	The study of how believers in different eras of the history of the church have understood various theological topics.
Philosophical Theology	The study of theological topics primarily through the use of the tools and methods of philosophical reasoning and information gained from nature and reason ("general revelation") apart from the Bible.
Practical Theology	The study of how to best apply theological truths to the life of the church and the world (including preaching, Christian education, counseling, evangelism, missions, church administration, worship, etc.).
Apologetics	The study of theology for the purpose of defending Christian teaching against criticism and distortion, and giving evidences of its credibility.

A concern for whole-Bible theology (i.e., systematic theology) can be seen in Paul's insistence that he did not shrink back from declaring "the whole counsel of God" (Acts 20:27), and in Jesus's Great Commission that the church should "make disciples of all nations" by "teaching them to observe all that I have commanded you" (Matt. 28:19–20). Jesus also uses this way of understanding the Bible as he takes his disciples through the Old Testament, showing that the whole Bible points to him (Luke 24:27, 44).

Area of Study	Technical Title
Method and Foundation	Prolegomena
The Bible	Bibliology
God	Theology Proper

Traditionally, the major topics covered in the study of theology (along with their technical terms) are:[10]

Area of Study	Technical Title
Humanity (or Man)	Anthropology
Sin	Hamartiology
Christ	Christology
Holy Spirit	Pneumatology
Salvation	Soteriology
Church	Ecclesiology
Last Things	Eschatology

ESSENTIAL VS. PERIPHERAL DOCTRINE

The ability to discern the relative importance of theological beliefs is vital for effective Christian life and ministry. Both the purity and unity of the church are at stake in this matter. The relative importance of theological issues can fall within four categories: (1) *absolutes* define the core beliefs of the Christian faith (e.g., the Trinity, the return of Christ); (2) *convictions*, while not core beliefs, may have significant impact on the health and effectiveness of the church (e.g., baptism, view of the Millennium); (3) *opinions* are less-clear issues that generally are not worth dividing over (e.g., worship style, timing of the Tribulation); and (4) *questions* are currently unsettled issues (e.g., when angels were created, the date of Christ's return). These categories can be best visualized as concentric circles, similar to those on a dartboard, with the absolutes as the bull's-eye.

Where an issue falls within these categories should be determined by weighing the cumulative force of at least seven

---

[10] This chart is from Thoennes, *Life's Biggest Questions*, 35; and "Biblical Doctrine: An Overview," 2506

considerations: (1) biblical clarity; (2) relevance to the character of God; (3) relevance to the essence of the gospel; (4) biblical frequency and significance (how often in Scripture it is taught, and what weight Scripture places upon it); (5) effect on other doctrines; (6) consensus among Christians (past and present); (7) effect on personal and church life; and (8) current cultural pressure to deny a teaching of Scripture. These criteria for determining the importance of particular beliefs must be considered in light of their cumulative weight regarding the doctrine being considered. For instance, just the fact that a doctrine may go against the general consensus among believers (see item 6) does not necessarily mean it is wrong, although that might add some weight to the argument against it. All the categories should be considered collectively in determining how important an issue is to the Christian faith. The ability to rightly discern the difference between core doctrines and legitimately disputable matters will keep the church from either compromising important truth or needlessly dividing over peripheral issues.

SOURCES IN DOING THEOLOGY

For the evangelical theologian, the foundational, authoritative source of our theology must be Scripture. As we have seen, Scripture is the "norming norm" of the entire theological process. God's revelation in his Word conclusively leads us to the ultimate Word of God in Christ, and provides the objective, authoritative revelation of God by which all other truth claims are judged. However, there are also at least three other sources we draw from as we "do theology." These are: reason, experience, and tradition.

THE ROLE OF REASON IN THEOLOGY

Since the Enlightenment (mid-seventeenth to mid-eighteenth centuries) there has been a growing belief in Western culture that truth is found primarily through the reasoning of the autonomous knower. Descartes's (1596–1650) famous statement, "I think, therefore I am," crowns individual human reason as the "king" of how we decipher truth (epistemology). This has led to unbridled confidence in human capacity to discover truth and reality without the need for anyone or anything outside of our own reason to tell us what is true. God and his Word are demoted in our learning. This way of thinking that took hold during the Enlightenment is called "naturalistic modernism." This led to "humanism," which has a highly optimistic view of human nature and looks solely to human reason to solve the problems of humanity.

For Enlightenment thinkers, knowledge was *certain*, *objective*, and *inherently good*, and the way you discovered it was primarily through reason. The goal of our thinking was objective, dispassionate knowledge. Think of the stoic Mr. Spock on *Star Trek*. The mere humans, so often ruled by their passions, would look to the stoic Spock to keep them on the path to understanding. He was the objective expert. For Enlightenment thinkers, knowledge was also inherently good. Thus, they were very optimistic. They felt that progress was inevitable, because this inherently good knowledge was obtainable.

This kind of thinking has profoundly shaped Western culture, but has increasingly come under attack, and, at least since the 1970s, the academy and even the general culture shifted away from naturalistic modernism. This shift has been called "postmodernism."

POSTMODERNISM

Postmodern thinkers have rejected the idea that autonomous human reason can get to truth or to an overarching metanarrative (a story that explains reality). In its place, postmodernism emphasizes "local narratives," which are by definition narrow in scope and authority and are created by "local communities." Postmodern thinkers believe that "truth is what your friends let you get away with saying."[11] Thus, postmodernism is, above all else, pluralistic and diverse. Kevin Vanhoozer describes it thus:

> Postmodern thinkers distinguish themselves from "modern" thinkers by their different stance towards reason: whereas the modern era is by and large characterized by an optimistic confidence in reason's ability to gain knowledge of the world and solve its problems, the postmodern thinkers profess a distrust in reason's abilities and a disbelief in reason's professed objectivity.[12]

Although a biblical understanding of truth and reality cannot embrace a postmodern perspective, it does provide a needed corrective to naturalistic modernism. Unchecked faith in human reason and the autonomous knower pushes the need for God out of our quest for truth. Postmodernism's critique forces us to acknowledge the limitations of unaided human reason. However, the postmodern turn did not lead back to depending on God's revelation to inform our reason, but to radical subjectivism and a relative view of truth. Objective truth, if it even exists, is not something we can discover. There is no hope of discovering a big story to explain reality; we are just left with subjective opinion.

Postmodernism has been no more helpful to Christianity than naturalistic modernism. Although postmodernism has helped us to think about the value of intuition, experience, and emotions in understanding reality, and has encouraged more intellectual humility, it led us into the lonely abyss of subjective relative experience as the only truth we will ever find. No wonder there is so much confusion and feelings of meaninglessness in our culture today.

The Christian worldview must put great value on human reason, but we must also be aware of the way sin has damaged our ability to reason well. Sin has greatly distorted our mental capaci-

---

[11] This quotation and similar versions of it has its origin in works by philosopher Richard Rorty.
[12] Kevin Vanhoozer, "Christ and Concept: Doing Theology and the 'Ministry' of Philosophy," in *Doing Theology in Today's World: Essays in Honor of Kenneth S. Kantzer*, ed. John D. Woodbridge and Thomas Edward McComiskey (Grand Rapids, MI: Zondervan, 1994), 128.

ties. We now "suppress the truth in unrighteousness" (Rom. 1:18 NASB). God's assessment of the fallen condition of the human mind will keep us from being overly confident in unaided human reason: "For although they knew God, they did not honor him as God or give thanks to him, but they became futile in their thinking, and their foolish hearts were darkened. Claiming to be wise, they became fools" (Rom. 1:21–22). "For the mind that is set on the flesh is hostile to God, for it does not submit to God's law; indeed, it cannot" (Rom. 8:7). Without the Spirit's help as he illumines our thinking according to the Scriptures, we will not be able to find true knowledge of God and his ways. Even for Christians, who have the Spirit but are not fully conformed to Christ's image yet, our reason cannot be totally trusted. But our reason is still a crucial part of our being created in the image of God and how we know God. Reason and logic come from God and are great and indispensable gifts as we seek to know him.

God invites his people to reason together with him: "Come now, let us reason together, says the LORD: though your sins are like scarlet, they shall be as white as snow; though they are red like crimson, they shall become like wool" (Isa. 1:18). New Testament authors often make important conclusions by drawing inferences from Old Testament teaching (e.g., Gal. 3:16). Jesus also leads us to make logical connections from our experiences. He urges us to draw comfort and confidence from the way God cares for birds and lilies, and leads us to conclude that he will certainly care for human beings, who are of far greater value to God (Matt. 6:26–30). Paul also reasons in this way when he writes, "He who did not spare his own Son but gave him up for us all, how will he not also with him graciously give us all things?" (Rom. 8:32). This way of reasoning from the "lesser to the greater" or "greater to the lesser" can be found often in the Bible (e.g., 1 Cor. 15:12–20). This should lead us to make eager use of our reasoning ability, even as we recognize how much we need God's revelation and illumination.

THE ROLE OF EXPERIENCE IN THEOLOGY

No one learns in a vacuum. We all bring our experiences, past and present, to the table when we learn. Sometimes these experiences predispose us to see truth and reality more clearly, and sometimes they have a distorting effect. However, all our experiences in some way contribute to shaping our theological understanding. Many great theologians have pointed to key experiences that profoundly shaped their theology. Since childhood, Jonathan Edwards hated what the Bible taught about the sovereignty of God. He explained his change of mind this way,

> But I remember the time very well, when I seemed to be convinced, and fully satisfied, as to this sovereignty of God, and his justice in thus eternally disposing of [dealing with] men, according to his sovereign pleasure. But never could give an account, how, or by what means, I was, thus convinced, not in the least imagining at the time, nor a long time after, that there was any extraordinary influence of God's Spirit in it but only that now I saw further, and my reason apprehended the justice and reasonableness of it. . . . And there has been a wonderful alteration in my mind, in respect to the doctrine of God's sovereignty, from that day to this; so that I scarce ever have found so much as the rising of an objection against it, in the most absolute sense.[13]

John Wesley did not plan to be converted the day he stepped into a meeting on Aldersgate Street, but as he listened to a reading of Luther's preface to the book of Romans, he was forever changed. Here is his description of his conversion experience: "I felt my heart strangely warmed. I felt I did trust in Christ, Christ alone, for salvation; and an assurance was given me that He had taken away my sins, even mine, and saved me from the law of sin and death."[14] These major changes of mind and heart that Luther,

---

[13] Jonathan Edwards, *Selections* (New York: Hill and Wang, 1962), 58–59.
[14] John Welsey, "I Felt My Heart Strangely Warmed," *Journal of John Wesley* (Chicago: Moody Press, 1951), Christian Classics Ethereal Library, accessed October 16, 2017, https://www.ccel.org/ccel/wesley/journal.vi.ii.xvi.html.

Edwards, and Wesley experienced were not merely intellectual de-
terminations but the culmination of years of emotional, intellectual, and circumstantial background that the Holy Spirit worked
within to bring about their transformation.

We are certainly rational beings, but we are much more than
that. God uses our experiences to help us understand and communicate his truth. God's revelation in the Bible through inspired
human authors brings their experiences into that inspiration process. The testimony of the authors of Scripture is based on their
eyewitness experience of God's mighty acts in history. We then gain
faith in God based on their experiences. The apostles spent time
with Jesus (1 John 1:1), and we can know Christ through their witness. True relationship with God is not based only in intellectual
assent but includes an experience of the living God as we are called
to "taste and see that the LORD is good" (Ps. 34:8).

However, subjective experience alone is not enough. Our reason
is always shaped and informed by our experiences, and the question we must always ask is, "How has my past experience shaped
my current understanding, and is my current understanding in line
with God's Word?" It can be a great challenge to shed the distorting effect that our experience has had on us. Many today think it
impossible but with the Bible informing our thinking, the help of
the Holy Spirit, and the correcting influence of diverse Christian
fellowship, it is indeed possible and necessary. To force our experiences on truth in a distorting way is idolatry for example. You may
have had a neglectful or abusive father, but to project that experience on your understanding of God's fatherhood dishonors God
and hinders your intimacy with him.

The Bible is clear that any experience we have that contradicts
biblical truth must be rejected and transformed by God's Word. "If
a prophet or a dreamer of dreams arises among you and gives you a
sign or a wonder, and the sign or wonder that he tells you comes to
pass, and if he says, 'Let us go after other gods,' which you have not

known, 'and let us serve them,' you shall not listen to the words of that prophet or that dreamer of dreams" (Deut. 13:1–3). The New Testament demands this kind of robust discernment and rejection of any experience that goes against God's Word. "But even if we or an angel from heaven should preach to you a gospel contrary to the one we preached to you, let him be accursed. As we have said before, so now I say again: If anyone is preaching to you a gospel contrary to the one you received, let him be accursed" (Gal. 1:8–9). Our experiences, even of good things, cannot ever be the final test of their truthfulness. Even dramatic spiritual experiences should not be the primary basis of our beliefs. Jesus teaches this clearly when he says,

> Not everyone who says to me, "Lord, Lord," will enter the kingdom of heaven, but the one who does the will of my Father who is in heaven. On that day many will say to me, "Lord, Lord, did we not prophesy in your name, and cast out demons in your name, and do many mighty works in your name?" And then will I declare to them, "I never knew you; depart from me, you workers of lawlessness." (Matt. 7:21–23; cf. Heb. 6:4–6)

All our experiences do have a crucial impact on our thinking, but experience itself does not have the final authority. The Word of God does.

This means that there are times when our feelings and experiences do not seem to be lining up with what God says is true. My (Erik's) experience seems to indicate that men are more sinful than women, and I have plenty of statistics to back up that claim (e.g., men commit over 80 percent of the violent crimes in the United States).[15] But the Bible tells me that men and women are equally sinful; thus I submit my experience to the Bible. There are times when God's ways do not seem wise or workable in the current day, but we trust his Word and obey him in spite of our experience. There exists

---

[15] "2014 Crime in the United States," FBI:UCR, accessed October 16, 2017, https://ucr.fbi.gov/crime-in-the-u.s/2014/crime-in-the-u.s.-2014/persons-arrested/main.

a common way of thinking today that to live out of conformity with how I *feel* is hypocrisy; but that is a wrong definition of hypocrisy. To live contrary to what I *believe* is hypocrisy. To live in conformity with what I believe, in spite of what I feel, isn't hypocrisy; it's integrity.[16] Authenticity should be defined by living according to our core beliefs and convictions, not by our feelings or experiences at the moment.

THE ROLE OF TRADITION IN THEOLOGY

"Tradition" refers to the entire process by which normative religious truths are passed from one generation to the next. Psalm 78:1–7 refers to tradition in this sense:

> Give ear, O my people, to my teaching;
>   incline your ears to the words of my mouth!
> I will open my mouth in a parable;
>   I will utter dark sayings from of old,
> things that we have heard and known,
>   that our fathers have told us.
> We will not hide them from their children,
>   but tell to the coming generation
> the glorious deeds of the LORD, and his might,
>   and the wonders that he has done.
>
> He established a testimony in Jacob
>   and appointed a law in Israel,
> which he commanded our fathers
>   to teach to their children,
> that the next generation might know them,
>   the children yet unborn,
> and arise and tell them to their children,
>   so that they should set their hope in God
> and not forget the works of God,
>   but keep his commandments.

---

[16] On this topic, Brett McCracken has written an excellent essay entitled "Has Authenticity Trumped Holiness?" The Gospel Coalition website, January 26, 2014, https://www.thegospel coalition.org/article/has-authenticity-trumped-holiness-2. He examines the importance of defining authenticity in the right way. His insightful book, *Uncomfortable* (Crossway, 2017), expands on this important theme.

Scripture is loaded with teaching based on an understanding of God's revelation passed on from previous generations. Paul grounds his teaching in the truth that he is passing on what he "received from the Lord" (1 Cor. 11:23). In addition to tradition within the Bible, there is also the collective teaching passed on by theologians through the centuries. This was defined in chapter 1 as historical theology.

So what role should tradition play in doing theology? Tradition in the Bible is viewed both positively and negatively. Jesus tends to denounce the use of "traditions of men" when they substitute for, or miss the point of, God's Word. Jesus strongly rebuked the Pharisees for their use of tradition: "'You leave the commandment of God and hold to the tradition of men.' And he said to them, 'You have a fine way of rejecting the commandment of God in order to establish your tradition! . . . Thus making void the word of God by your tradition that you have handed down. And many such things you do'" (Mark 7:8–9, 13). Paul also condemns the distorting use of tradition: "See to it that no one takes you captive by philosophy and empty deceit, according to human tradition, according to the elemental spirits of the world, and not according to Christ" (Col. 2:8).

The Bible also recognizes a vital part that tradition should play. The writers of the New Testament saw their role as largely passing on what they had received (1 Cor. 11:23), and those receiving their message were commended for passing on what they had received: (cf. 1 Cor. 11:2; 15:3–11). We, along with Timothy, are commanded to receive and pass on the teaching we've received: "Follow the pattern of the sound words that you have heard from me, in the faith and love that are in Christ Jesus. By the Holy Spirit who dwells within us, guard the good deposit entrusted to you" (2 Tim. 1:13–14). Of course, apostolic teaching that is being passed on has its origin and authority in Christ. But what about tradition that is not inspired by Scripture?

Basically, there have been two ways of viewing church tradition: one, represented by the Roman Catholic and Eastertn Orthodox traditions, and the other within the tradition that was recovered in the Protestant Reformation. Both of these views appreciate and have an important place for tradition and creeds in doing theology. But the Roman Catholic and Eastern Orthodox perspectives have put church tradition and Scripture on essentially an equal plane, while the Protestant understanding puts tradition under scrutiny and ultimate authority of Scripture.

The Protestant view holds to the Reformation belief in *Sola Scriptura* (Scripture alone). That is the view held by the authors of this book (based on the functional absolutes regarding the Bible that were presented in chapter 1). While we must have deep knowledge of, and respect for, the teachings of the church throughout the centuries, it must be Scripture that constantly holds the ultimate authority.

Even though a Protestant evangelical understanding of *Sola Scriptura* maintains the Bible as the final judge in all matters of theology and Christian ethics, we should not neglect the vital insights tradition provides. We must seek the correction and clarity that theologians from the past offer. Both present-day teachers and those from past centuries can be great gifts to God's people (Eph. 4:11).

The study of historical theology shows that God has chosen to use frail humans and events to refine our understanding of his Word over time. We need to recognize that we are all located in a particular time and place and therefore are influenced by that location in history. We can see great Christians who believed things that we recognize now were not consistent with Scripture. This should lead to humility regarding our inability to understand theology without blind spots that come with our current historical context. We can become aware of those blind spots and do all we can to rid ourselves of them, but we can be sure we will always have some until we no longer "see through a glass darkly" (1 Cor. 13:12).

To gain greater clarity about what Scripture teaches, we have much to learn from how past theologians have interpreted texts of Scripture. We can learn from their errors as well as their helpful insights. Theologians have been willing to die for what they were convinced was an accurate understanding of God's Word. This does not mean their interpretations were always correct, but it does show us how strongly they believed that you could rightly understand the truth and that it really mattered.

Too often today we have little knowledge of our past, so we fail to learn from it. The Enlightenment and evolutionary theory have led many to believe in unlimited and unrelenting human progress. This leads to believing that what is new is always better, and that more recent formulations of the exegetical meaning of biblical texts and of systematic theological understanding are always more advanced and superior to earlier ones. C. S. Lewis calls this "chronological snobbery."[17] We can assume that any way of the thinking that came before our "enlightened" day is necessarily inferior. J. I. Packer describes this arrogance this way: "The newer is the truer. Only what is recent is decent. Every shift of ground is a step further. And every latest word must be hailed as the last word on its subject."[18]

Although theologians do not give us inspired Scripture, we desperately need their insights through the centuries as they reflected on the teaching of Scripture. We also need to glean insights from living brothers and sisters in the church, especially those from different cultures and backgrounds and traditions than ours. Only then will we have the kind of sharpening we need to understand God's Word accurately.

At the center of all our efforts to use reason, experience, and

---

[17] C. S. Lewis, *Surprised by Joy* (Harcourt, Brace, Jovanovich, 1966), 207–8.

[18] J. I. Packer, "Is Systematic Theology a Mirage? An Introductory Discussion," in *Doing Theology in Today's World: Essays in Honor of Kenneth S. Kantzer*, ed. John D. Woodbridge and Thomas Edward McComiskey (Grand Rapids, MI: Zondervan, 1991), 21.

tradition, we must continue to hold the Bible as our final authority. It alone is the Word of God to us. With all the value of reason, experience, and tradition, evangelical theologians nevertheless affirm the ultimate and final authority of canonical Scripture. That must remain the final authority and ultimate judge of all of Christian theology and ethics.

> All Scripture is breathed out by God and profitable for teaching, for reproof, for correction, and for training in righteousness, that the man of God may be complete, equipped for every good work. (2 Tim. 3:16–17)

FAITH DEVELOPMENT IN ACADEMIA

In academic environments it can seem as if nothing is certain. Academics love to discuss, debate, and argue, and controversial books sell better. So areas of disagreement can often get most of the attention in a college setting. There is a vital place for debate and good arguing, not as an end in itself—but as a means of arriving at solid truth. Often our students will say things such as, "We have been studying the Bible and theology for ages, and still no one agrees on anything." They can start to feel hopeless about their ability to interpret even one passage of the Bible correctly. They can be seized with "exegeti-phobia."

Actually, Christians committed to the ultimate authority of the Bible have had amazing unity of belief on the major issues of the faith across the ages. For most of our history, Christians have agreed on the core doctrines of the faith and have been willing to die for those beliefs. Also, it is important to remember that God has decided to reveal himself to frail creatures like us, and has entrusted the refinement of that revelation to us. This can be a painfully slow and messy process, but God likes to show himself in the messiness of relationships in time and history because that makes it real and relational.

We can also have wrong expectations of a kind of mathematical certainty for the things we believe about God. Theological truth is rational, but it is also relational. It does not provide scientific certainty, but in key ways it provides an even deeper kind of truth and certainty. It is more like my being sure of my wife's love for me; I have evidence for it, but not the kind that solves math equations. We believe in Christ in part because he explains *everything* so much better than anything else does. As C. S. Lewis said, "I believe in Christianity as I believe that the sun has risen—not only because I see it, but because by it I see everything else."[19]

Academic environments appear artificial because your life is dominated by intense attainment of ideas, and you can seldom get to live out those ideas or test them out in daily life. Ideas will seem tenuous until you get to put them into action. Jesus said that putting his teaching into practice brings validation to it, "If anyone's will is to do God's will, he will know whether the teaching is from God or whether I am speaking on my own authority" (John 7:17).

When things get uncertain and confusing, try to get away from the academic world in which you live, and look for very simple, very real service opportunities—service like caring for an elderly or developmentally disabled person, or doing manual labor for your local church or go on a mission trip to work with the poor. When things seem uncertain and confusing, keep considering the man, Jesus, and asking yourself, "What about him is not true?" And when you doubt if you really believe in him, ask yourself if you ever do things just because he told you to. If so, it is highly likely you truly believe in him.[20]

The first theology professor I (Erik) ever had was Tim Phillips, who was a fantastic example of a theologian who was a true disciple of Christ, and it was a joy to see him and his wife, Sandy,

---

[19] C. S. Lewis, *Is Theology Poetry?* (Samizdat University Press, 1945), 15.
[20] A novel that brilliantly makes the case for what we are saying here, and that I (Erik) frequently recommend to my students when they are struggling with assurance of their faith, is: George McDonald, *Thomas Wingfold, Curate*, Christian Classics Ethereal Library, accessed October 16, 2017, https://www.ccel.org/ccel/macdonald/thomaswingfold.

follow Christ in daily life. Tim made it home to heaven the week of his fiftieth birthday, but anyone who had him for class (as I did four times!) frequently heard him repeat two statements that summarized our entire endeavor in biblical and theological studies. The first one was: "The role of the church is to display eschatological (end-time) realities now!" Who God is, what he has done, and what he will do when Jesus returns to make all things new, must shape the nature and ministry of the church, so that she becomes a trailer of coming attractions for all the world to see. The church should be the place that is showing Jesus's power and presence even before his kingdom finally comes in fullness and the King is worshiped by every nation on earth. The other thing Tim would often say was, "The final question of theology is, 'Am I being obedient to Jesus today?'" All our study of the Bible and theology should lead to knowledge of God that translates into expressing our love for Christ and his lordship in simple, daily obedience.

"Jesus answered . . . , 'If anyone loves me, he will keep my word, and my Father will love him, and we will come to him and make our home with him. Whoever does not love me does not keep my words. And the word that you hear is not mine but the Father's who sent me'" (John 14:23–24). God has spoken.

QUESTIONS FOR REFLECTION

1) When you determine what is true and real, how do you decide which voices are most trustworthy? What kind of authority do you think the Bible deserves in your life? Do you think the Bible explains reality as you know it in a truthful, or at least plausible, way?

2) The Bible says that the heavens declare the glory of God. Do you see God's glory in creation? Do you see God's glory in the face of Jesus Christ? What about Jesus is not true, good, or beautiful in your perspective?

3) Where have you learned your methods for interpreting the Bible? How did the nature of the Bible and methodology for interpreting it presented in chapter 2 differ from how you approached the Bible in the past?

4) If one views the Bible as both a divine and human book, how will that effect the way you interpret it and understand it?

5) What has your attitude been in the study of the Bible and theology? Has anything in this book helped to increase your appreciation for doctrine?

6) What would you know about God if all you had was general revelation (creation)? How does special revelation (God's Word) help you interpret creation and contribute to your understanding of God?

7) If there were any errors in the Bible, even small ones, how would that affect your trust in it? If God inspired Scripture with errors, what would that imply about God? If you believe that the Bible and everything it affirms is true, how should that influence your attitude toward it?

8) Can you see how all of life's greatest problems originate in a faulty understanding of who God is? Can you think of any greater reason for all the problems in the world?

9) Are you able to see that Jesus is at the center of the Bible and the whole point of it? Have you ever trusted him as your Savior?

GLOSSARY

ANE. This is an acronym for the "Ancient Near East" world, providing background information on the practices and beliefs of Israel's neighboring nations such as the Egyptians and the Mesopotamians.

Apologetics. The study of theology for the purpose of defending Christian teaching against criticism and distortion, and giving evidences of its credibility.

Audience context. Refers to the experience and situation of the immediate audience of those who originally heard or read a biblical text.

Biblical studies. An academic discipline that seeks to understand the Bible as God intended when he inspired its human authors.

Biblical theology. The study of scriptural revelation based on the historical framework presented in the Bible. It is the study of the storyline and thematic emphases of Scripture as a whole, and/or of limited portions of Scripture. It is the systematic presentation of biblical themes, teachings, and doctrines. Biblical theology has been for many the basic mission of showing the historical progression of revelation in the Bible.

Continuity. Continuity emphasizes the similarities and continuation of the messages of the Old and New Testaments, especially with reference to theological systems, hermeneutics, salvation, the law of God, the people of God, and kingdom promises.

Covenantal nomism. Covenantal nomism is a view developed in the New Perspective on Paul that expresses the idea that the works of the law are not a means of entering into the covenant, but they are "badges" for staying in the covenant. Adherents believe that the works of the law function as proper responses to one's election and membership in God's covenant community.

Cultural context. Refers to the specific way of living in a particular society, including the political, social, religious customs, and worldview of a given society.

Diachronic approach. A diachronic approach to the backgrounds of the Bible looks into the chronological events in biblical history.

Discontinuity. Discontinuity emphasizes the differences of the messages of the Old and New Testaments, especially with reference to theological systems, hermeneutics, salvation, the law of God, the people of God, and kingdom promises.

Doctrine. Doctrine (from the Latin *doctrina*) is a codification of beliefs or a body of teachings on a specific topic, such as the Trinity, the virgin birth of Jesus, the deity and humanity of Jesus, the atonement, the second coming of Christ, the church, etc.

Exegesis. The process of seeking to determine the correct meaning of a particular passage of Scripture.

Extra-biblical materials. This includes archaeology (which is the history of excavation), history, and geography of the land and their bearings upon the Old and New Testaments. This also includes studies of the Qumran community and Dead Sea Scrolls, its belief and practices, and the relationship of these findings to Old and New Testament studies.

Hermeneutics. The attempt to establish methodological principles of interpretation, especially of written texts.

Higher criticism. Higher criticism can be divided into two main categories: historical criticism and literary criticism. Historical criticism analyzes the formation of the biblical text; this discipline consists of three movements: source, form, and redaction criticism. Literary criticism builds off historical criticism and analyzes the features of the biblical text in its final form. Since there are three components to a literary text (author, reader, and the text itself), each method of literary criticism has one of these components as its basis for understanding the meaning of the text.

Historical theology. The study of how believers in different eras of the history of the church have understood various theological topics.

History of interpretation. This entails going outside of the Bible and viewing the way that the Bible has been interpreted throughout history.

Intertestamental period. Also referred to as Second Temple Judaism, this is the period from the end of the Old Testament to the dawn of the New Testament.

Lower criticism. Lower criticism analyzes the preservation and transmission of the biblical text in the discipline called text criticism.

Masoretic Hebrew text. From the Hebrew term *masoreth* (tradition), this is the traditional Hebrew text of the Jewish Bible, assembled and codified and supplied with diacritical marks to enable correct pronunciation.

Morphology. The study of the classes and structures of words, such as noun declension and verb structure.

New covenant. The new covenant was promised in the Old Testament (Jer. 31:31–34; cf. Ezek. 36:26–32) and fulfilled in the New Testament (Luke 22:20; Heb. 8:6–13) as God provided salvation from sins through the sacrifice of Christ on the cross, and produced a regenerated heart and empowerment through the work of the Holy Spirit in the lives of those who yielded themselves to Jesus as their Savior and God.

New perspective on Paul. This is a varied study and reinterpretation of the apostle Paul's view of the Old Testament law and the nature of justification within Second Temple Judaism, so that our view of Judaism today does not misrepresent or generalize Judaism.

New Testament studies. The mission of New Testament studies is to help students develop skills in the areas of interpretation of the books of the New Testament, the historical-cultural setting, and biblical theology. The intended outcome is for students to better understand God's written Word in order to apply it to the development of a distinctly Christian worldview that they would live out in daily life and ministries in the presence of the living Word of God.

Old covenant. The expression "old covenant" is generally used to refer to the solemn vow God made with Israel in which God called the nation to obey him and keep his law, and in return God would protect and bless them (Deut. 30:15–18; 1 Sam. 12:14–15).

Old Testament studies. Old Testament studies on the most basic level aim to acquaint students with the life, customs, and thought of the Hebrew people and their neighbors in the biblical and related periods. It studies the literary genre, structure, and themes of each book and the purpose of the writers, as well as selected introductory and critical issues (e.g., authorship, dating, setting) and crucial problems (e.g., prophecy). On a more advanced level, students are given instruction in the original languages with an accurate foundation in Hebrew and Aramaic grammar, syntax, and exegesis so that their expositions of the English translations will reflect a sound basis of interpretation.

Pentateuch. Pentateuch means "five books" in Greek, and refers to the first five books of the Bible—Genesis, Exodus, Leviticus, Numbers, and Deuteronomy—which Jews call the Torah.

Philosophical Theology. The study of theological topics primarily through the use of the tools and methods of philosophical reasoning and information gained from nature and reason ("general revelation") apart from the Bible.

Practical Theology. The study of how to best apply theological truths to the life of the church and the world (including preaching, Christian education, counseling, evangelism, missions, church administration, worship, etc.).

Second Temple Judaism. Refers to the same basic time period as the Intertestamental period, from the rebuilding of the temple after the Jewish exile up to the destruction of the temple in AD 70, but with regard for Jewish sensibilities.

Septuagint (LXX). From the Latin *septuaginta*, "seventy," the Septuagint is a Greek translation of the Hebrew Scriptures undertaken in Alexandria, Egypt, in the third or second centuries BC by Jewish scholars and adopted by Greek-speaking Christians. The tradition is that seventy (or seventy-two) Jewish scholars were the translators behind the Septuagint, abbreviated with the Roman numeral LXX (70).

Suzerain covenant. A suzerain covenant takes place between a powerful ruler and a dependent vassal group. The ruler promises benefits and protection to the vassal group, and by the vassal group remaining loyal to the suzerain through law-keeping, the covenant is maintained.

Synchronic approach. This approach to the backgrounds of the Bible analyzes culture and highlights the manners, customs, institutions, and principles that were relevant to a particular time and environment.

Syntax. The arrangement and interrelationship of words in larger constructions than words, such as sentences and paragraphs.

Systematic Theology. The effort to summarize and synthesize the overall teaching of the Bible so that it can be meaningfully applied to our lives. A study that answers the question, "What does the whole Bible teach us today about a given topic?"

Type. A "type" indicates that an event or person in the Old Testament is a foreshadowing of what God will do in the future.

Typology. Centers on the idea of correspondence between people, events, and institutions throughout the historical activity of God.

World context. Refers to concepts and experiences that are applied universally.

RESOURCES FOR FURTHER STUDY

GENERAL

Allison, Gregg R. *50 Core Truths of the Christian Faith: A Guide to Understanding and Teaching Theology*. Crossway, 2018.

Douglas, J. D. *The New Bible Dictionary*. Third edition. Wheaton, IL: Tyndale, 1996.

———. *The New International Dictionary of the Christian Church*. Revised edition. Grand Rapids, MI: Zondervan, 1978.

Elwell, Walter, ed. *Evangelical Dictionary of Theology*. Second edition. Grand Rapids, MI: Baker, 2001.

Erickson, Millard, J. *Christian Theology*. Grand Rapids, MI: Eerdmans, 1985.

———. *The Concise Dictionary of Christian Theology*. Revised Edition. Wheaton, IL: Crossway, 2001.

Grudem, Wayne. *Systematic Theology: An Introduction to Biblical Doctrine*. Grand Rapids, MI: Zondervan, 1994.

House, Wayne. *Charts of Christian Theology and Doctrine*. Grand Rapids, MI: Zondervan, 1992.

Packer, J. I. *Concise Theology: A Guide to Historic Christian Beliefs*. Wheaton, IL: Tyndale House, 2001.

THE BIBLE

Carson, D. A., and John Woodbridge, eds. *Hermeneutics, Authority, and Canon*. Grand Rapids, MI: Zondervan, 1986.

———. *Scripture and Truth*. Grand Rapids, MI: Zondervan, 1983.

Geisler, Norman L., ed. *Inerrancy*. Grand Rapids, MI: Zondervan, 1980.

Hayden, Dan. *Did God Write the Bible?* Wheaton, IL: Crossway, 2010.

Helm, Paul. *The Divine Revelation: The Basic Issues*. Westchester, IL: Crossway, 1982.

Henry, Carl F. H. "Bible, Inspiration of." In *EDT*, pp. 145–49.

Packer, J. I. *"Fundamentalism" and the Word of God*. London: Inter-Varsity Press, 1958.

Warfield, Benjamin Breckinridge. *The Inspiration and Authority of the Bible*. New York: Kessinger Publishing, 2008.

Wenham, John W. *Christ and the Bible*. London: Tyndale Press, 1972.

White, James R. *Scripture Alone: Exploring the Bible's Accuracy, Authority and Authenticity*. Minneapolis, MN: Bethany House, 2004.

THE WORD OF GOD

Frame, John M. *Perspectives on the Word of God*. Eugene, OR: Wipf & Stock, 2000.

Ward, Timothy. *Words of Life: Scripture as the Living and Active Word of God*. Downers Grove, IL: IVP Academic, 2009.

THE INERRANCY OF SCRIPTURE

Beale, G. K. *The Erosion of Inerrancy in Evangelicalism: Responding to New Challenges to Biblical Authority*. Wheaton, IL: Crossway, 2008.

Packer, J. I. "Scripture." In *NDT*, pp. 627–31.

———. "Infallibility and Inerrancy of the Bible." In *NDT*, 337–39.

CLARITY OF SCRIPTURE

Carson, D. A. *Exegetical Fallacies*. Grand Rapids, MI: Baker, 1984.

Hubbard, Robert L., William W. Klein, and Craig L. Blomberg. *Introduction to Biblical Interpretation*. Waco, TX: Word Books, 1993.

Packer, J. I. "Infallible Scripture and the Role of Hermeneutics." In *Scripture and Truth*. Edited by D. A. Carson and John Woodbridge. Grand Rapids, MI: Zondervan, 1983, pp. 325–56.

THE DOCTRINE OF GOD

Frame, John. *The Doctrine of God: A Theology of Lordship*. Phillipsburg, NJ: P&R, 2002.

Charnock, Stephen. *The Existence and Attributes of God*. Reprinted edition. Evansville, IN: Sovereign Grace Book Club, n.d., pp. 69–180. (First published, 1655–1680.)

Morgan, Christopher W. and D. A. Carson. *The Love of God*. Wheaton, IL: Crossway, 2016.

Packer, J. I. *Knowing God*. London: Inter-Varsity Press, 1973, pp. 13–37.

Piper, John. *Desiring God*. Portland, OR: Multnomah, 1986.

———. *The Pleasures of God*. Portland, OR: Multnomah, 1991.

Sproul, R. C. *The Holiness of God*. Carol Stream, IL: Tyndale, 2000.

Tozer, A. W. *The Knowledge of the Holy*. New York: Harper and Row, 1961.

Ware, Bruce A. *God's Greater Glory: The Exalted God of Scripture and the Christian Faith*. Wheaton, IL: Crossway, 2004.

THE TRINITY

DeWeese, Garrett, Donald Fairbairn, Scott Horrell, and Bruce Ware. *Jesus in Trinitarian Perspective: An Introductory Christology*. London: B&H Academic, 2007.

Kostenberger, Andreas J. and Scott R. Swain. *Father, Son and Holy Spirit: The Trinity and John's Gospel*, New Studies in Biblical Theology series. Downers Grove, IL: IVP Academic, 2008.

Letham, Robert. *The Holy Trinity: In Scripture, History, Theology and Worship*. Phillipsburg, N J: P&R Publishing, 2005.

McGrath, Alister E. *Understanding the Trinity*. Grand Rapids, MI: Zondervan, 1988.

Owen, John. *Communion with the Triune God*. Edited by Kelly M. Kapic and Justin Taylor. Wheaton, IL: Crossway, 2007.

Reeves, Michael. *Delighting in the Trinity: An Introduction to the Christian Faith*. Downers Grove, IL: InterVarsity Press, 2012.

Sanders, Fred. *The Deep Things of God: How The Trinity Changes Everything*. 2nd edition. Wheaton, IL: Crossway, 2017.

Ware, Bruce. *Father, Son, & Holy Spirit: Relationships, Roles, & Relevance*. Wheaton, IL: Crossway, 2005.

HUMANITY

Hoekema, Anthony A. *Created in God's Image*. Grand Rapids, MI: Eerdmans, and Exeter: Paternoster, 1986, pp. 1–111.

Piper, John and Justin Taylor. *Sex and the Supremacy of Christ*. Wheaton, IL: Crossway, 2005.

MAN AND WOMAN

Andreades, Sam. *enGendered: God's Gift of Gender Difference in Relationship*. Wooster, OH: Weaver, 2015.

Kassian, Mary A. *Women, Creation, and the Fall*. Westchester, IL: Crossway, 1990.

Piper, John and Wayne Grudem, eds. *Recovering Biblical Manhood and Womanhood: A Response to Evangelical Feminism*. Wheaton, IL: Crossway, 2006.

SIN AND EVIL

Carson, D. A. *How Long, O Lord? Reflections on Suffering and Evil*. Grand Rapids, MI: Baker, 1990.

Owen, John. *Overcoming Sin and Temptation: Three Classic Works by John Owen*. Edited by Kelly M. Kapic and Justin Taylor. Wheaton, IL: Crossway, 2006.

Piper, John and Justin Taylor, eds. *Suffering and the Sovereignty of God*. Wheaton, IL: Crossway, 2006.

Plantinga Jr., Cornelius. *Not the Way It's Supposed to Be: A Breviary of Sin*. Grand Rapids, MI: Eerdmans, 1995.

THE PERSON OF CHRIST

Anselm. *Why God Became Man: And The Virgin Conception and Original Sin*. Translated by Joseph M. Colleran. Albany, NY: Magi, 1969.

Athanasius. *On the Incarnation*. Translated by CSMV. New York: Macmillan, 1946.

Harris, Murray J. *Jesus as God*. Grand Rapids, MI: Baker, 1992.

Macleod, Donald. *The Person of Christ*. Contours of Christian Theology. Downers Grove, IL: InterVarsity Press, 1998.

THE ATONEMENT

Demarest, Bruce. *The Cross and Salvation: The Doctrine of Salvation*. Wheaton, IL: Crossway, 2006.

Morris, Leon. *The Apostolic Preaching of the Cross*. 3rd edition. Grand Rapids, MI: Eerdmans, 1965.

Murray, John. *Redemption Accomplished and Applied*. Grand Rapids, MI: Eerdmans, 1955.

Owen, John. *The Death of Death in the Death of Christ*. Carlisle, PA: Banner of Truth, 1959. (Includes the excellent introductory essay by J. I. Packer.)

Packer, J. I. and Mark Dever. *In My Place Condemned He Stood: Celebrating the Glory of the Atonement*. Wheaton, IL: Crossway, 2008.

Stott, John R. W. *The Cross of Christ*. Leicester and Downers Grove, IL: InterVarsity Press, 1986.

THE RESURRECTION

Ladd, George E. *I Believe in the Resurrection of Jesus*. Grand Rapids, MI: Eerdmans, 1975.

Wright, N. T. *Surprised by Hope: Rethinking Heaven, the Resurrection, and the Mission of the Church*. New York: HarperOne, 2008.

THE ASCENSION

Dawson, Gerrit Scott. *Jesus Ascended: The Meaning of Christ's Continuing Incarnation*. Phillipsburg, NJ: P&R, 2004.

Chester, Tim and Jonny Woodrow. *The Ascension: Humanity in the Presence of God*. Fern, Ross-shire, Scotland: Geanies House, 2013.

THE HOLY SPIRIT

Cole, Graham. *Engaging with the Holy Spirit: Real Questions, Practical Answers*. Wheaton, IL: Crossway, 2008.

———. *He Who Gives Life: The Doctrine of the Holy Spirit*. Wheaton, IL: Crossway, 2007.

Ferguson, Sinclair B. *The Holy Spirit*. Contours of Christian Theology. Downers Grove, IL: InterVarsity Press, 1997.

Packer, J. I. *Keep in Step with the Spirit*. Old Tappan, NJ: Revell, 1984.

Stott, John R. W. *Baptism and Fullness: The Work of the Holy Spirit Today*. Downers Grove, IL: InterVarsity Press, 1964.

SALVATION

Barrett, Matthew. *Salvation by Grace: The Case for Effectual Calling and Regeneration*. P&R, 2013.

Boice, James, M. and Philip G. Ryken. *The Doctrines of Grace: Rediscovering the Evangelical Gospel*. Wheaton, IL: Crossway, 2009.

Clotfelter, David. *Sinners in the Hands of a Good God: Reconciling Divine Judgment and Mercy*. Chicago: Moody Publishers, 2004.

Packer, J. I. *Evangelism and the Sovereignty of God*. London: Inter-Varsity Press, 1961.

Smedes, Lewis B. *Union with Christ: A Biblical View of the New Life in Jesus Christ*. 2nd edition. Grand Rapids, MI: Eerdmans, 1983.

Watson, Thomas. *The Doctrine of Repentance*. Carlisle, PA: Banner of Truth, 1987.

THE CHURCH

Bavinck, Herman. *Reformed Dogmatics, vol. 4*. Grand Rapids, MI: Baker Academic, 2008.

Bonhoeffer, Dietrich. *Life Together*. San Francisco: HarperOne, 1954.

Clowney, Edmund. *The Doctrine of the Church*. Philadelphia: P&R, 1969.

Dever, Mark. *Nine Marks of a Healthy Church*. Wheaton, IL: Crossway, 2004.

Dever, Mark and Jamie Dunlop. *The Compelling Community: Where God's Power Makes a Church Attractive*. Wheaton, IL: Crossway, 2016.

Frame, John M. *Worship in Spirit and Truth*. Phillipsburg, NJ: P&R, 1996.

Ladd, George Eldon. "The Kingdom and the Church." In *A Theology of the New Testament*. Grand Rapids, MI: Eerdmans, 1974, pp. 105–19.

Moore, Russell D. *The Kingdom of Christ: The New Evangelical Perspective*. Wheaton, IL: Crossway, 2007.

Saucy, Robert. *The Case for Progressive Dispensationalism*. Grand Rapids, MI: Zondervan, 1993.

Baxter, Richard. *The Reformed Pastor*. Carlisle, PA: Banner of Truth, 1979.

Strauch, Alexander. *Biblical Eldership: An Urgent Call to Restore Biblical Church Leadership*. Littleton, CO: Lewis and Roth, 1986.

HEAVEN AND HELL

Gerstner, John H. *Repent or Perish*. Ligonier, PA: Soli Deo Gloria, 1990.

Gomes, Alan W. *40 Questions about Heaven and Hell*. Grand Rapids, MI: Kregel, 2017.

Blamires, Harry. *Knowing the Truth about Heaven and Hell*. Knowing the Truth series. Edited by J. I. Packer and Peter Kreeft. Ann Arbor, MI: Servant, 1988.

GENERAL INDEX

academia, faith development in, 107–9
Ancient Near East (ANE), 55; ANE law, 55, 55n39
Apocrypha, Jewish, 55, 65
archaeology, 47
atheism, 17

backgrounds, use of in biblical studies, 53–56; audience context, 54; cultural context, 53–54; diachronic approach to backgrounds, 54; and the Jewish writings from the Intertestamental period, 55–56; synchronic approach to backgrounds, 54–55; world context, 53, 53n31
Barr, James, 51
Bible, the: clarity of, 34–35; inaugurated fulfillment of, 61; inerrancy of, 33–34; inspiration of, 33; Jesus's view of, 36–38; narrative of, 18–19; negative and positive views of tradition in the Bible, 104; sufficiency of, 35–36; unity of, 18, 72–73. See also Bible, the, three horizons of
Bible, the, three horizons of, 76, 76n124; the horizon of biblical authors' perspectives on God's activities in history, 77–78; the horizon of contemporary significance, 78–79; the horizon of a unified record of God's activities in history, 76–77
biblical discernment, development of, 90
biblical studies, 18, 38–39; and the divine-human nature of the Bible, 75–76. See also biblical studies, contemporary issues in; biblical studies, overview of the methods of; New Testament studies; Old Testament studies
biblical studies, contemporary issues in, 50; ancient and future Israel, 61–64; critical tools of biblical criticism, 56–58; languages of the Bible, 50–53; new perspective on Paul, 70–72; quest for the historical Jesus, 67–70; relationship of the Old and New Testaments, 59–61; Second Temple Judaism, 64–67; theological reading of the Bible, 72–75; use of backgrounds, 53–56

biblical studies, overview of the methods of, 80; application and communication, 83–84; biblical and systematic theology, 83; historical-cultural contexts, 82; the interpretive problem, 83; lexical, grammatical, and syntactical contexts, 82–83; literary contexts, 82; original languages and translation, 81–82; outlining, 83; texts and Scripture, 80–81; textual criticism, 81
biblical studies, sub-disciplines of. See hermeneutics; historical analysis; interpretation, history of; literary analysis; theological analysis
biblical theology, themes of: covenant relationship, 74; promise and fulfillment, 74; salvation history, 73–74; Trinitarian rule of faith, 74–75
biblical theology studies, attitudes necessary for, 19–26; fear and worship of God, 20–21; having an eagerness to learn and discover mysteries and challenges, 24; heartfelt gratitude and joy, 24–25; humility, 21–23; obedience, 24; prayerful dependence on the Holy Spirit for guidance, 23–24
Bornkamm, Gunther, 69
Brunner, Emil, 89
Bultmann, Rudolf, 68

Calvin, John, 87–88
Charnock, Stephen, 88
Chicago Statement on Biblical Inerrancy, 34–35
consumerism, 19
corporate solidarity, 60–61
correspondence, in history, 61
Cotterell, Peter, 51
"covenantal nomism," 71
covenants: of God with Israel (the old covenant), 44; in reference to the Old and New Testaments, 44; suzerainty covenants, 55
creation, Genesis accounts of, 44–45
critical tools, 56–61; development of during the Enlightenment, 56; feminist criticism, 58; form criticism, 57–58; higher criticism, 57; historical criticism, 57, 58;

liberationist criticism, 58; literary criticism, 57, 58; lower criticism and text criticism, 56–57; narrative criticism, 58; post-structuralism, 58; reader-centered criticism, 58; reader-response criticism (audience criticism), 58; redaction criticism, 57, 58; rhetorical criticism, 58; source criticism, 57; structuralism, 58
Cyrus the Great, 64

David, 47; and Bathsheba, 79
Dead Sea Scrolls, 47, 55–56, 67
deism, 17
Descartes, René, 97
doctrine, 85; criteria for essential versus peripheral doctrine, 95–96; Reformation, 72
doxology, 20
Dunn, James, 71–72

Edwards, Jonathan, 100, 101
Enlightenment, the, 56, 97, 106
entertainment, mentality of, 19
equivalency: dynamic equivalency, 81; formal equivalency, 81
Essenes, 66, 67
evolutionary theory, 106
exegesis, art/science of, 81

Fuchs, Ernst, 69

geography, 47
God, 91, 99; activities of throughout history, 76–78; attributes of, 29; basic assumptions concerning, 17–18; glory of, 89; grace of, 21; incomprehensibility of, 28–30; intimacy with, 86; knowledge of, 27–28, 30–31, 86–87; the personal nature of God's revelation, 93; relationship with, 92; sovereignty of, 100; transcendence and immanence of, 32. See also God, functional absolutes of
God, functional absolutes of, 26; general revelation, 27–28; God exists and has revealed himself, 26–27; the incomprehensibility of God, 28–30; special revelation, 27, 28
Great Commandment, 92
Great Commission, 92, 94
Green, Joel B., 76n124
Greidanus, Sidney, 76n124

Henrie, Mark, 46
hermeneutics, 41–44, 80; development of a consistent hermeneutical method, 41–42; further training in methods of biblical interpretation, 42–43; hermeneutical assumptions, 60–61; as a subset of philosophy, 43–44; and the wise interpretation of literary forms, figures of speech, and genres used in the Bible, 43
historical analysis, 46–47; extra-biblical materials used in, 47
Holy Spirit, 91, 99, 104
humanism, 97

Institutes of the Christian Religion (Calvin), 87–88
interpretation, history of, 49–50
Intertestamental history. See Second Temple Judaism
Israel: ancient and future Israel, 61–64; as the "people of God," 61–62, 62n69. See also Judaism

Jeremiah, 47
Jesus, 79, 91, 92, 99, 104; glory of, 89; knowledge of, 89; as the living Word of God, 75
Jesus, historical, quest for, 67–70; the new quest (1950–1980s), 69; the old quest (seventeenth to the mid-twentieth centuries), 68–69; third quest (late twentieth century), 69
Jesus Seminar, 69
Jewish Antiquities (Josephus), 65
Job, 20
Josephus, 55, 65
Judaism, 47, 71, 72. See also Second Temple Judaism
Justification and the New Perspectives on Paul (Waters), 72
justification by faith, 70–72

Käsemann, Ernst, 69
knowledge, objective, 97

language, as an instrument of communication: and the flexibility of language, 53; and language at the utterance level, 52; and the location of language within culture, 51–52
Lewis, C. S., 106, 108
Life of Jesus Critically Examined, The (Strauss), 68
linguistics: grammatical analysis, 52; interdisciplinary emphasis on New Testament Greek and linguistics, 50; structural and descriptive approach to, 50–51. See also language, as an instrument of communication
Linguistics and Biblical Interpretation (Cotterell and Turner), 51

literary analysis, 48, 82
Luther, Martin, 70, 100

Maccabees, books of, 65–66
Martin, Ralph, 47
Masoretic text (MT), 57
Midrash, 61
Mishnah, the, 55, 67
modernism: "naturalistic modernism," 97; postmodernism, 97–99
Moses, 47

Nestle-Aland, 57
New Testament, 102, 104; continuity between the Old and New Testaments, 63; discontinuity between the Old and New Testaments, 63–64; divine authorship of, 44; "interpreted history" literary form of, 78; relationship of the Old and New Testaments, 59–61; uniqueness of, 46. See also New Testament use of the Old Testament, interpretative methods of
New Testament studies, 45–46
New Testament use of the Old Testament, interpretative methods of: hermeneutical assumptions, 60–61; Jewish exegetical methods, 61; text form, 60

Old Testament, 62n69; continuity between the Old and New Testaments, 63; discontinuity between the Old and New Testaments, 63–64; divine authorship of, 44; as foundational for understanding the New Testament, 44–45, 65; relationship of the Old and New Testaments, 59–61; setting of in the Ancient Near East (ANE), 55. See also New Testament use of the Old Testament, interpretative methods of
Old Testament studies, 44–45
orthopraxy, 20

Packer, J. I., 106
Paul, 47, 94; new perspective concerning, 70–72; on the unity of believers, 42–43
"People of the Book," 46
Perrin, Norman, 69
Pesher, 61
Peter, 47
Pharisees, 66, 67
Philips, Sandy, 108–9
Philips, Tim, 108–9
Philo of Alexandria, 55
pragmatism, 19
pride, 22–23
Psalms, literary analysis of, 48
Pseudepigrapha, 55, 66

Quest for the Historical Jesus, The (Schweitzer), 68
Qumran community, the, 47, 56

Reformation, the, 72, 105
rule of faith, 74–75

Sadducees, 66, 67
salvation history, 73–74
sanctification, 92
Sanders, E. P., 71, 72
Schweitzer, Albert, 68
Scripture. See Bible, the
Second Temple Judaism, 55, 64–67
Semantics of Biblical Language (Barr), 51
sin/sinfulness, 89–90; effects of, 29–30
Sola Scriptura, 105
Stendahl, Krister, 71
Strauss, David Friedrich, 68

Talmud, the, 55, 67
theological studies, 18; attitudes necessary for the study of, 19–26
theology, 20; applied theology, 19; biblical theology, 48–49, 72–75, 83; categories of systematic theology, 89; historical theology, 105–6; how to study theology, 91; Johannine theology, 49; New Testament theology, 49; Old Testament theology, 49; as "Queen of the Sciences," 87; the role of experience in, 100–3; the role of reason in, 96–97; the role of tradition in, 103–7; source of evangelical theology, 96; systematic theology, 83, 92, 94; theological analysis, 48–49; theological method, 92–93; theological process, 93–95; theology as relational-transformational truth, 85–90; why study theology, 85–90
Thielicke, Helmut, 22
Tozer, A. W., 87
tradition, in the church: Eastern Orthodox tradition, 105; Protestant tradition, 105; Roman Catholic tradition, 105
Trinity, the, 91–92
Turner, Max, 51
typology, 73

United Bible Societies, 57

Vanhoozer, Kevin, 98

Waters, Guy Prentiss, 72
Wesley, John, 100, 101
Whyte, Alexander, 21
world context, and metaphor, 53, 53n31
Wright, N. T., 71, 72

SCRIPTURE INDEX

Genesis
1	17
1:1–28	76
17:7	62
49:10–11	67

Exodus
3:14–15	32
6:6–7	62
32:16	75

Leviticus
4	45

Numbers
24:17	67

Deuteronomy
4:2	35
6:6–7	34
12:32	35
13:1–3	102
29:29	30, 36

2 Samuel
7:28	33

Job
26:14	28
42:5–6	20

Psalms
12:6	33
14:1	27
19:1	27
19:7	34
19:7–8, 10–11	26
19:7–9	35
22	61
22:1	37
34:8	101
51:16–17	79
78:1–7	103
113:4–6	32
119:14, 103–105	26
119:18	23
119:42	33
139:17	25
145:3	28

Proverbs
30:5	33
30:5–6	35

Isaiah
1:18	99
6:5	20
7:14	45, 59, 60
7:17	59
9:6–7	45
11:1–9	67
42:1	61
42:6	62
55:8–9	29
57:15	32
65:16	91

Jeremiah
31:31–34	62

Joel
2:28	61

Matthew
1:20–25	45
1:22–23	59, 60
1:23	79
2:1	52
4:1–11	37
5:12	37
5:17–18	37, 38
5:18	65
5:21–48	37
6:26–30	99
6:33–34	19
7:21–23	102
11:23–24	37
12:1–8	61
12:3, 5	34
12:41–42	37
19:1–12	37
19:4	34
19:4–6	37
21:42	34
22:31	34
22:37	38
22:37–40	85
22:39	37
24:35	38
24:37–39	37
26:54	37
27:39–46	61
27:46	37
28:19–20	85, 94
28:20	79, 92

Mark
3:13–19   38
7:1–13   37
7:8–9, 13   104
8:31   37
12:30   92
12:31   92

Luke
1:4   77
4:25–27   37
5:8   20
10:25–26   37
11:50–51   37
24:13–17, 44–47   37
24:26–27   60
24:27, 44   94

John
1:1, 14   75
7:17   24, 108
8:31–32   92
8:56–58   37
10:9   42
10:11   59
14:6   91
14:10, 24   38
14:23–24   109
15:1   59
15:15   25
15:26   91
16:12–14   38
16:13   91
17:17   33, 92
20:31   78

Acts
1:21–22   60
2:17   61
2:24–36   60
3:12–16   60
4:8–11   60
5:29–31   60
17:25   22
17:27–28   32
20:27   94
26:16–18   38

Romans
1:18   99
1:18, 21, 25   92
1:18–26   30
1:19–20   27
1:19–21   27
1:21–22   99
2:14–15   27
3:28   70
4:2–5   53
7:12, 22   70
8:7   99

8:14   36
8:19–23   45
8:32   99
9:25   62
11:29   64
11:33–34   29
11:33, 36   20
12:2   92
15:4   44

1 Corinthians
1:31   22
2:12–13   38
2:14–16   23
4:7   22
8:1   22
10–12   54
11:2   104
11:23   104
12:28   35
13:12   106
15:3–11   104
15:12–20   99
15:49   45

2 Corinthians
1:20   74
4:6   89
5:17   45
6:16–17   62

Galatians
1:8–9   102
2:16   71
3:16   99
3:28   42
4:4–5   45
5:16, 18, 25   36
6:16   63

Ephesians
1:16–18   24
2:12   63
4:11   35, 105

Philippians
3:10   89

Colossians
2:8   104

1 Thessalonians
2:12   45

2 Thessalonians
2:11–13   92

1 Timothy
1:17   21

2 Timothy
1:13–14   104
2:7   34

2:15	43, 81
3:15	35
3:16	33, 75
3:16–17	35, 107

Titus

1:2	33

Hebrews

5:11–6:3	90
5:12–6:1	90
6:4–6	102
10	45

James

1:18	92
2:17–20	53
2:19	23

1 Peter

1:23	92
2:2	38
2:9–10	62
5:5	23

2 Peter

1:20–21	33
1:21	58
3:16	34

1 John

1:1	101
5:13	78

Revelation

19:13	75
20:11–21:1	76
21:7	62
22:18–19	36

RECLAIMING THE CHRISTIAN INTELLECTUAL TRADITION SERIES

CHRISTIAN WORLDVIEW
A STUDENT'S GUIDE

Philip Graham Ryken

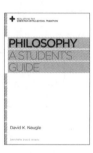

PHILOSOPHY
A STUDENT'S GUIDE

David K. Naugle

THE GREAT TRADITION OF CHRISTIAN THINKING
A STUDENT'S GUIDE

David S. Dockery & Timothy George

ETHICS AND MORAL REASONING
A STUDENT'S GUIDE

C. Ben Mitchell

THE LIBERAL ARTS
A STUDENT'S GUIDE

Gene C. Fant Jr.

POLITICAL THOUGHT
A STUDENT'S GUIDE

Hunter Baker

LITERATURE
A STUDENT'S GUIDE

Louis Markos

ART AND MUSIC
A STUDENT'S GUIDE

Paul Munson & Joshua Farris Drake

THE NATURAL SCIENCES
A STUDENT'S GUIDE

John A. Bloom

PSYCHOLOGY
A STUDENT'S GUIDE

Stanton L. Jones

HISTORY
A STUDENT'S GUIDE

Nathan A. Finn

MEDIA, JOURNALISM, AND COMMUNICATION
A STUDENT'S GUIDE

Read Mercer Schuchardt

For more information, visit **crossway.org**.